Shared Success

How Teamwork Leads to Winning in Life

by
Dr. Rajan Gupta, MD

Table of Contents

Introduction:
Weaving Individual Success into Collective Triumph

The fabric of success, intricate and resilient, is woven from the threads of individual efforts and united by the loom of collective endeavor. This tapestry is not created by solitary artisans, but by a cadre of diverse hands, each contributing a unique color, texture, and strength. The essence of triumph lies not merely in the aggregation of singular achievements, but in the alchemy of personal victories that, when intertwined, forge an unbreakable chain of achievement. The following chapters are dedicated to unraveling this alchemy, providing a blueprint for harnessing the power of togetherness in forging paths laden with win-win scenarios.

At the heart of every endeavor that stands the test of time is the indomitable spirit of teamwork. It invites us to look beyond our personal horizons and to find, within the collective purpose, a greater sense of meaning and fulfillment. The chapters herein dissect the anatomy of effective teams, from the foundational principles of trust and transparency to the intricate dance of leadership and followership. Each segment meticulously constructs a paradigm where the success of one is a triumph for all, reinforcing the notion that the zenith of individual potential is often reached through the support of a scaffold built by many hands.

As we embark on this journey together, each page will serve as a stepping stone toward a profound realization; that our own aspirations are irrevocably linked to the shared goals of those who accompany us. With every chapter, a new strand of wisdom will be woven into the reader's consciousness, cultivating an environment where motivation and commitment bloom in the fertile soil of collaboration. Let us then begin the journey of weaving individual success into collective triumph, embarking on a transformative path where together, we achieve more than we ever could alone.

Chapter 1:
The Foundation of Teamwork

In the fertile soil of collaboration, the seeds of individual excellence can sprout into a flourishing tree of collective triumph; this transformative process rests upon a bedrock known as the foundation of teamwork. At the core, it's the harmonious interplay of diverse minds and talents unified by a common aim that propels any group toward its pinnacle of success. To lay the groundwork for such an alliance, it is imperative to understand the essence of working together—the silken threads that bind separate strands into a tapestry of unparalleled strength. By fostering an environment steeped in trust and transparency, and celebrating the rich tapestry woven from mutual respect for diversity, teams craft a shared vision that becomes their guiding star. As we delve into the fundamental principles that construct the base upon which great teams are built, we are reminded of the power inherent in shared endeavors and the beauty of many voices singing a single melody, creating a symphony of achievement that resounds with the potential for infinite possibilities.

The Essence of Collaboration

As we delve deeper into the framework of teamwork, it's crucial to unearth the essence of collaboration. The fabric of teamwork is woven not just through the connection of goals, but by the interlocking threads of individual skills and contributions. Each person brings unique qualities to the team, and through collaboration, they harmonize into a symphony of collective achievement.

At its core, collaboration is the alchemy that transforms multiple perspectives into a singular vision of success. It transcends the mere pooling of efforts; it is about leveraging each other's strengths to reach heights that would be unattainable alone. This seamless integration is the bedrock upon which teams construct their foundation.

Consider the image of a mosaic, an art form that beautifully encapsulates the spirit of collaboration. Each piece, unique in shape, color, and texture, contributes to the overall masterpiece. Without the contribution of each individual tessera, the final piece would be lesser for it.

To foster true collaboration within a team, there must be an ethos of open communication. Opinions should not only be heard but valued, and members must be encouraged to contribute irrespective of their role. In such a nurturing environment, the hesitancy to share innovative ideas diminishes, sparking an inferno of creativity and ingenuity.

Indeed, one of collaboration's greatest strengths is its potential to unlock innovative solutions. When diverse minds congregate with a willingness to intertwine their insights and expertise, the result is often a breakthrough that propels the team forward in ways previously unconceived.

A thriving collaborative environment also demands a sense of mutual respect among team members. This respect fosters a supportive atmosphere where individuals feel valued and important. It's a place where people don't just work side by side, but genuinely work together, celebrating each other's contributions and pulling each other up in times of need.

Integral to fostering collaboration is the establishment of common goals. While individual objectives can guide personal achievement, collective aims synchronize efforts, ensuring that every action contributes to a unified outcome. This shared vision becomes the compass that guides every decision and strategy within the team.

Collaboration is not merely about the harmony of working together; it also involves the willingness to contend with the discordance of differing opinions. This dissonance, challenging as it might be, is essential, as it prevents the stagnation of ideas and fosters the growth necessary for a dynamic team.

One could view collaboration as a dance of both lead and follow, where leadership fluidly transfers among team members according to the task at hand. This dynamic not only maximizes the use of each member's particular skill set but also bolsters a sense of ownership and responsibility throughout the team.

Moreover, effective collaboration harbors an understanding that success is collective, and failure is not an orphan. Teams that embrace this notion aren't demoralized by setbacks; instead, they view them as shared learning opportunities that strengthen their collective resolve and agility.

At its most sublime, collaboration results in a win-win scenario, where the team's achievements translate into personal satisfaction for its members. Every individual's success story is a chapter in the team's grand narrative—a testament to the powers of togetherness.

To maintain the essence of collaboration, teams should foster ongoing dialogue, actively and consistently immerse themselves in each other's ideas, and remain adaptable to shifting roles and responsibilities. The sustainability of collaborative efforts hinges on this constant nurturance.

Collaboration, therefore, is more than a mere strategy; it's a mindset, a culture that needs to be cultivated and cherished. It respects the intricacies of human interaction and holds the promise of unlocking limitless potential when individuals come together with common purpose and passion.

In summary, collaboration is the lifeblood of any effective team. It is the process through which individual talents are amplified by the collective, where innovation is born from the confluence of diverse thoughts, and where shared victories become the milestones of mutual growth. The next step in our journey examines the principles that beautifully scaffold strong, collaborative teams, ensuring that each piece of the masterpiece fits perfectly in place, resulting in a majestic tableau of teamwork.

Key Principles for Building Strong Teams

In the realm of teamwork, the foundation is built upon principles that when woven together, create the fabric of a strong and effective team. Embracing these key principles is essential in fostering a culture where collective triumph eclipses individual success while still valuing the unique contributions of each member.

One cardinal principle in team building is the development and nurturing of trust and transparency. Trust acts as the cornerstone upon which strong teams are constructed. It is the assurance team members require to fully engage, share ideas freely, and take meaningful risks without fear of ridicule or reprisal. Transparency complements trust by promoting an open environment where intentions are clear, and actions are understandable, leaving little room for doubt and suspicion.

Mutual respect and diversity are equally critical in building strong teams. Respect ensures each team member feels valued, acknowledging that everyone, regardless of role or experience level, contributes to the team's success. Diversity goes beyond mere representation; it leverages a rich tapestry of backgrounds, experiences, and perspectives, which can lead to more creative solutions and better decision-making.

Another foundational element in team building is the embracement of common goals and a shared vision. A team aligned behind a common purpose moves forward cohesively, turning individual efforts into a powerful collective force. A shared vision provides a roadmap, guiding the team's energies towards the desired future state and aligning their day-to-day actions with long-term objectives.

Furthermore, communication plays an irreplaceable role in building strong teams. Effective communication fosters understanding and minimizes misunderstandings, establishing a rhythm that keeps the team in sync. It's the conduit through which ideas flow and the platform upon which members can voice concerns, share triumphs, and collaborate on challenges.

Commitment to the team's goals is a driving force that cannot be overlooked. When individuals commit, they are making a promise to themselves and others to give their best towards the collective aim. This galvanizes the team, creating a robust and unwavering force that can push through obstacles and maintain focus on achieving set targets.

Cultivating an environment where members are encouraged to take initiative and assume responsibility is key to strengthening a team's capability. Empowering team members fosters a culture of leadership and accountability at all levels, allowing the team to leverage the strengths and insights of each individual effectively.

The principle of adaptability ensures that a team remains effective in the face of change. The ability to pivot and respond to new circumstances is essential in a fast-paced and ever-evolving environment. Teams that cultivate adaptability are better equipped to handle unforeseen challenges and can convert potential setbacks into opportunities for growth.

Moreover, integrating a mindset that values conflict as a catalyst for innovation and creativity is another principle for strong team building. When teams approach clashes not as dead-ends but as springboards for improvement, they transform tensions into energy that propels the team forward.

Building a culture that celebrates success and recognizes individual and team efforts is also fundamental. Celebration and recognition create a positive feedback loop, reinforcing the behaviors that lead to success and fostering a climate where members feel appreciated and motivated to continue their contributions.

As teams navigate their journey, gauging performance and embracing a culture of continuous feedback and improvement is essential. This principle ensures that teams can evaluate their dynamics, identify areas for enhancement, and implement strategies to elevate their performance, always striving from good to great.

Lastly, the principle of embodiment calls for every team member to personify the values and ideals of the team. When members lead by example, they reaffirm the team's core beliefs and set a standard for others to follow, creating a self-sustaining ecosystem of excellence and unity.

The power of togetherness within a team cannot be overstated. It is in the binding of these principles that teams find the strength to innovate, overcome challenges, and reach heights unattainable by individuals working alone. Each principle interlocks with the next, forming a solid structure that allows for individual growth while propelling the team to collective success.

Embrace these principles wholeheartedly, and watch as a group of individuals transforms into a cohesive, unstoppable force. A strong team is more than the sum of its parts; it is a beacon of possibility, a testament to the power of unity, and the harbinger of shared triumphs.

The foundation of teamwork is not merely about building a team, but about sowing the seeds of togetherness that flowers into enduring success. In this way, the team can truly create a win-win scenario for all its members, leading passionately towards a common horizon of collective accomplishment.

Trust and Transparency

Within the sphere of collaboration are principles of paramount importance that pave the way toward collective achievement. True cohesion emerges not out of mere proximity or shared tasks but, significantly, from a deep-rooted sense of trust. This sentiment is cultivated when actions and motives are as clear as a crystalline stream, revealing the pebbles of intent and commitment beneath its surface. To articulate this principle is to affirm that every member of the group operates with disclosed intentions and openly communicated thoughts, eschewing hidden agendas.

The value of transparency in a team setting cannot be understated; it stands as the stabilizing scaffold for trust. When team members disclose their progress, share information freely, and provide honest feedback, a fabric of reliability is woven. Each strand of candor and forthrightness strengthens the collective fabric, ensuring that when pressure mounts, the team does not fray but, instead, rallies together with conviction. This openness fosters a secure environment where vulnerability is not shunned but embraced as an avenue for genuine connections and growth.

However, trust does not emerge overnight; it is a plant that requires the steady sunlight of transparency to grow. Team members must consistently demonstrate their reliability by meeting commitments and taking responsibility for their actions. This reliability creates predictability, and in turn, predictability forges an environment where trust can flourish. It is within such an environment that individuals feel empowered to take risks and innovate, confident in the knowledge that their teammates are supportive anchors and not hidden shoals.

In the collective journey towards success, each action taken in the spirit of transparency is akin to a beacon, signaling to others the direction and progress of the team. Stakeholders and members alike are drawn to such beacons, for they know that where there is light, there can be no deceit. Leadership, in this context, must be exemplary, actively practicing transparency and encouraging it through recognition and reinforcement of honest efforts. Leaders set the tone, and when their actions exude integrity, teams naturally emulate these practices.

In the end, the bond of trust fortified by transparency is not merely an abstract virtue but a tangible foundation upon which the edifice of collective success is built. This unshakable trust engenders a sense of security, fuels teamwork, and becomes the currency of collaboration. As each individual operates within this trustworthy paradigm, they contribute to a synergy where the sum of the team's accomplishments is far more potent than the isolated triumphs of solitary endeavor. Thus, transparency is not just the pathway to trust; it is the thoroughfare to unparalleled togetherness and, ultimately, collective victory.

Mutual Respect and Diversity

It is axiomatic that the bedrock of effective collaboration is founded on mutual respect and diversity. As we delve into this critical component of building cohesive teams, it is essential to recognize that respect isn't merely tolerance; it's an active appreciation for the unique attributes and perspectives each member brings to the table. Fostering an environment where these qualities are celebrated not only enriches the team but also serves as a catalyst for unparalleled creativity and problem-solving. In such a space, members feel valued, heard, and empowered to contribute their very best.

Imagine the immense potential of a team that not only accepts but leverages the varying backgrounds, skills, and viewpoints of its members. This rich tapestry of human experience can render a group robust and dynamic, offering a wealth of options when facing challenges. When we integrate the array of personal narratives and wisdoms into our collective decision-making process, we harness the strength that inherently lies in diversity. It's not just about including different people but about creating an ecosystem where everyone's voice can not only echo but also resonate and shape the team's destiny.

Respect is a two-way street, and in an environment of genuine mutual respect, every individual not only receives honor but also returns it in kind. It's an ongoing exchange, one that demands attentiveness and acknowledgment. When people feel respected, they are more likely to engage wholeheartedly, share their unfiltered insights, and remain committed during turbulent times. This respect extends beyond the internal team dynamics to include how the team interacts with external partners and stakeholders, embracing differences while forging ahead towards the shared vision that unites them.

Crucial to harnessing diversity is the commitment to inclusivity. It's not enough to merely invite diversity into the room; we must also provide the space for it to thrive. This means actively dismantling barriers that keep certain voices on the fringes and deliberately crafting opportunities for all to shine. Adopting inclusive practices is a testament to an organization's dedication to actualizing the principles of respect and cherishing the broad spectrum of human expression. When inclusivity becomes the norm, teams become hotbeds for innovation, reflection, and evolution.

In summary, the convergence of mutual respect and diversity within a team sets a powerful stage for collective excellence. It elevates the group beyond the sum of its parts to a high-functioning unit, enriched by its differences and made resilient by its collective respect. This is where the alchemy of team synergy truly unfolds, producing results that not just meet the baseline but soar above and beyond, lifting each individual and the team into a sphere of continuous achievement and impactful success.

Common Goals and Shared Vision

Within the fabric of successful teams lies an essential thread: the alignment of common goals and a shared vision. This deep-seated coherence serves not only as a compass, guiding team members towards a unified destination but also as a foundation for the spirit of camaraderie that fuels their collective journey. Imagine a crew at sea, each member rowing rhythmically in concert, driven by a shared intention to reach the same port.

Yet, it is not enough to simply declare a composite goal; intention and understanding must weave through the hearts and minds of each individual. A shared vision is cultivated through ongoing communication, where every member has a voice. This inclusive process ensures that the team's objectives are not only accepted but also personally resonant. As members invest their passion into these common aspirations, their dedication transforms from obligatory to heartfelt, turning their efforts into contributions made with conviction and a clear sense of purpose.

The synergy created by a collective vision is a potent force. When harnessed, it streamlines efforts, eliminating the friction of disjointed objectives. It's like a well-orchestrated symphony in which each instrument plays its part, contributing to an exquisite harmony more beautiful than the sum of its parts. This unity does not stifle individual creativity but rather amplifies it. In an environment that seeks synchrony of intent, diverse ideas thrive, as every suggestion is considered a piece upon the shared canvas of achievement.

A team aligned in purpose purges the path of ambiguity, making strides with assured footfalls. Setting and reviewing goals periodically ensures the vision remains vivid and relevant, adapting with the agility of a sapling to the shifting winds of circumstance. Clarity of purpose fortifies the team against the turbulence of challenges, as the shared vision becomes the lighthouse during stormy weathers, guiding the collective vessel back to its course.

Acknowledging and celebrating small victories accumulated on the way to larger triumphs is crucial in sustaining motivation and commitment. As team members witness the fruits of their labor and appreciate each other's contributions, their investment in the shared vision deepens. In essence, it's the shared victories, the small moments of collective pride and accomplishment, that cement the bond between individuals, transforming a gathering of people into an unstoppable force with a singular, pulsating heart. When everyone is moving forward together, success takes care of itself.

Chapter 2:
The Strength of Shared Goals

As we delve into the second chapter, a powerful theme emerges with the exploration of shared goals within the framework of collaborative success. The mosaic of individual talents and the cultivation of a synchronized vision are not merely idealistic notions but the bedrock upon which great achievements are built. When a group commits to a common objective, an energy akin to an indefatigable force is unleashed, propelling every member toward greatness. In such a dynamic, the individual's ambitions do not shrink; instead, they crystallize, aligning with the team's journey, ensuring that as one person ascends, the collective does too. This alignment ushers in a robust structure where individual strengths bolster collective need and every victory belongs as much to the unit as it does to the person. This chapter not only underscores the vitality of unity but also serves as a compass orienting us towards recognizing that true power is found in the hearts of those who dare to dream together.

Defining a Unified Vision

The journey toward shared success is akin to navigating a vast sea. Individual goals act like the compasses held by each crew member, guiding them in their unique duties. Yet, for the collective voyage to be victorious, all compasses must point toward a common horizon—a unified vision. Discovering this horizon and aligning everyone's efforts to its direction is the cornerstone of collective triumph.

A unified vision is not simply a goal or a destination; it's fundamentally the soul of the team's quest. It's the vivid image that inspires action and ignites passion within each team member. This vision goes beyond the confines of individual aspirations to encompass the broader impact and potential of the team's success.

To define such a vision, one must begin with an honest and open dialogue. These conversations are the bedrock upon which the team's aspirations are built. Here, each individual's voice is heard, and each viewpoint is valued to ensure the resulting vision is not merely an echo of one member but a chorus of the entire collective.

A unified vision brings clarity, distilling an array of individual objectives into a singular purpose. It's a beacon that offers guidance when obstacles arise and decisions need to be made. It also serves as a rallying point, a shared dream that every team member is driven to turn into reality.

By defining this vision, we instill a sense of belonging in everyone. Each member's contributions are no longer separate threads but integral strands woven into the grand tapestry of the team's objectives. This interconnectedness reinforces the notion that although the path may be challenging, the journey is shared.

It is paramount, therefore, that a unified vision be ambitious yet attainable, a perfect balance between audacity and realism. It should stretch the capabilities of the team without straining them to a breaking point. This equilibrium encourages growth and maintains motivation, as progress becomes visible and the vision attainable.

Let's not mistake a unified vision with enforced uniformity. It celebrates the diverse strengths and talents of each team member, understanding that the mosaic of abilities is what propels the team toward this shared future. Integrating these differences into one clear image is the art of creating a vision that is genuinely unified.

Achieving such unity requires unwavering commitment from leadership as well as from the ranks. It calls for a measure of sacrifice, with individuals sometimes setting aside their personal goals for the greater good of the team. This sacrifice, however, is not a loss but an investment in a larger, shared success.

Once set, a unified vision becomes the imperative against which all actions are measured. It facilitates alignment, ensuring that every strategy, every decision, every innovation moves the team closer to its collective aspirations. This does not limit creativity but rather channels it toward a purpose that transcends individual achievement.

Crafting a unified vision is an iterative process. It accommodates the flow of time and the onset of unforeseen circumstances. It is bound to adapt, yet its core remains unchanged, much like a tree whose branches may sway but whose roots are steadfastly anchored.

To engrain this vision within the fiber of the team's consciousness, it must be communicated with conviction and consistency. The narrative of the shared future should be woven into everyday interactions and decisions so that it permeates the culture of the team entirely.

Moreover, to maintain its relevance and power, a unified vision must be celebrated and revisited often. With every milestone reached, the team should reflect upon their vision, recognize their progress, and rekindle their commitment to the shared journey ahead.

It's also worth noting that the vibrancy of a unified vision lies in its ability to inspire beyond the immediate team. It carries the potential to influence other teams, stakeholders, and the broader community, painting a picture of positive change and collective advancement.

In conclusion, defining a unified vision is an endeavor of profound import. It binds the team in an unbreakable chain of purpose, with every link crucial to the integrity of the whole. It highlights that while individual excellence is commendable, it is the convergence of these excellences towards a common dream that creates an unstoppable force—a team that can triumph over the greatest of challenges and reach the furthest of shores.

The next chapter will further analyze the role of individual contributions, and how they can be balanced against team needs to ensure that the vision that is so carefully crafted here is brought to fruition in unity and strength. Together, we advance toward success not as solitary travelers, but as a cohesive team, driven by a vision that is as much ours individually as it is ours together.

The Role of Individual Contributions

In the panorama of collective ambition, each individual plays a key role that is as crucial as it is unique. When identifying the vigor that undergirds shared goals, it becomes apparent that individual contributions are the indispensable threads in the fabric of teamwork.

A unified vision may be the cornerstone of triumphant collaboration, yet it is the personal expertise and enthusiasm that members bring which supply the color, texture, and strength to that foundation. Individual contributions stem not only from expertise or skill but also from passion, creativity, and responsible autonomy that allow a group to navigate the path to success.

The essence of collaboration is in appreciating that each person carries a reservoir of potential. This potential, when channeled toward a unified purpose, amplifies the collective capability. A group comprised of diverse individuals, each harnessing their strengths, creates a dynamic synergy that propels everyone forward. Such a team is like a well-conducted orchestra, where each instrument, playing its part, contributes to the splendor of the whole.

Trust and transparency, as previously discussed, set the stage for individuals to bring their best selves to the table. With a secure, open environment, team members are more inclined to take initiative, share innovative ideas, and express concerns—elements that are indispensable for progress and facing challenges.

There's a balance to be struck between individual autonomy and the needs of the group. The beauty of this equilibrium is that it allows for personal growth within the framework of team objectives, leading to an enriched collective journey and individual fulfillment.

In acknowledging each individual's importance, it becomes imperative for teams to ensure that voices are heard and contributions are not only welcomed but sought. Therein lies the art of fostering a culture where every member feels valued and knows that their work is instrumental to the team's achievements.

Diversity within a team is a wellspring of innovation and breakthroughs. Each team member's unique background, perspective, and skill set add to a rich tapestry of thought that can address challenges with a multi-faceted approach. Embracing these differences and leveraging them for the team's projects results in outcomes that are often greater than the sum of their parts.

Maintaining motivation and dedication to the group cause, even amidst hindrances, is tightly linked with how individual efforts are recognized and celebrated. Those acknowledgments are powerful motivators and reassure team members that their daily contributions have real impact and worth.

As leaders and peers within a group, fostering a spirit of mentorship and supportive feedback is invaluable. Encouraging and guiding others to stretch their capabilities not only develops individual talent but also fortifies the team's overall competence.

When it comes to responsibilities and tasks, clear definition and fair distribution ensure that no individual is overburdened, and all can invest their full capabilities into their roles. Alignment of individual responsibilities with strengths and interests is a strategic approach that can enhance both performance and satisfaction.

Furthermore, it is crucial to provide opportunities for team members to hone their skills and contribute their expertise in meaningful ways. Continuous learning opportunities and challenging projects can serve as catalysts for individual growth and, by extension, team development.

Adaptability is a shared responsibility. As individuals embrace change and demonstrate flexibility by learning from setbacks and adjusting quickly, the group becomes more resilient. This adaptability not only weathers storms but also can harness the forces of change for the team's advantage.

Lastly, as team members navigate their respective roles, the ethos of creating win-win situations becomes all the more relevant. Achieving more together relies on crafting solutions that acknowledge and address individual needs alongside those of the collective.

In summation, the role of individual contributions within the strength of shared goals stands as a testament to the transformative power of togetherness. When each member of a team understands and executes their role with commitment and excellence, the team not only achieves its objectives but transcends expectations, moving from good to great in a symphony of concerted effort.

Every individual contribution, no matter how modest it may seem, threads the needle through the cloth of shared purpose, weaving a tapestry that tells a story of unity, perseverance, and triumph.

Balancing Individual Strengths with Team Needs

In navigating the delicate balance between honing individual talents and addressing collective goals, there lies a profound opportunity for transformation. Within the context of a team, each member brings their unique strengths, experiences, and abilities. To achieve harmony, we must ensure these personal attributes not only coexist but also complement and enhance the group's dynamic.

Consider for a moment the symphony orchestra: each musician is a master of their instrument, yet it's only when they play in concert, attuned to the ensemble's collective needs, that they create an exquisite musical experience. Similarly, in teams, blending singular capabilities with team objectives leads to elevated performance and outcomes that transcend individual efforts.

It begins with self-awareness. Individual members need to have a profound understanding of their strengths and the wisdom to acknowledge areas where others excel. By embracing their niche, each person can contribute to the team in the most effective manner. Leaders within the team play a crucial role in recognizing and cultivating these strengths, positioning each member where they can shine and contribute meaningfully.

However, focusing solely on individual strengths without considering the team's needs can lead to an imbalance. Without a central, unifying goal, even the most talented members may pull in conflicting directions, diluting the potency of their collective efforts. Therefore, a shared vision is imperative—a north star guiding all members toward a common destination.

The quintessence of synergy can be felt when individual strengths are not just recognized but seamlessly integrated into the fabric of team strategy. This requires flexibility from the members to sometimes step out of their comfort zones and adapt their personal skills for the greater good. The team's strategy may necessitate shifts in roles or adopting new skills, which, in turn, contributes to each member's personal growth and the team's versatility.

Communication is the conduit for this transformation. An environment where members openly discuss roles, expectations, and concerns paves the way for mutual understanding and effective collaboration. Regular check-ins and feedback loops help maintain alignment, ensuring that individual efforts coalesce into the team's objectives, much like individual threads woven into a strong and complex tapestry.

When a team successfully marries individual strengths to team needs, the result is a thriving, dynamic unit that is more creative, agile, and robust. Team members feel valued and invested, knowing that their contributions are critical to the team's success. This investment fosters a deeper commitment and willingness to support one another, propelling the team towards shared achievements.

Of course, achieving this balance is not without its challenges. It requires ongoing effort and intentionality from all members. At times, it calls for difficult decisions to be made, perhaps redistributing tasks or redefining goals to better harness the collective strengths. These moments, though challenging, are catalysts for growth and innovation.

In essence, the balance between individual strengths and team needs is a dynamic interplay, a dance of particles each attuned to the rhythms of a greater whole. As teams strive towards this synergy, they discover that their collective power is not in uniformity but in the diverse and potent mosaic of their members' gifts, channeled towards a singular, shared purpose.

Thus, let teams embark on this journey, valuing each person's uniqueness, fostering an environment where those strengths contribute to a larger, concerted effort, and above all, ensuring the unity of purpose remains paramount. In this balance lies the secret not only to a successful team but to a legacy of collaborative excellence that resonates far beyond the sum of its parts.

Chapter 3:
Communication: The Heartbeat of Teamwork

In the fabric of teamwork, clear and compassionate communication threads itself as the most vital strand, pulsating with the potential to synchronize a myriad of hearts and minds. When teammates articulate their ideas, expectations, and concerns with clarity and sincerity, they build an invisible bridge that carries the entire team towards a shared destination of success. Nurturing an environment where everyone's voice is not only heard but also valued, creates a symphony of diverse thoughts harmonizing into innovative solutions. This chapter delves into the art of crafting open communication channels that can weather the storms of conflict and thrive in the calm of consensus. Here, we will explore the vitality of each spoken word and unspoken sentiment in fortifying the ties that bind a team, ensuring the heartbeat of communication remains strong, rhythmic, and resonant with the echoes of collective triumph.

Crafting Open and Effective Communication

In the intricate dance of collaboration, communication is the melody that synchronizes the varied steps of individuals into a cohesive performance. Delving deeper into the importance of this element within the symphony of teamwork, it's essential to understand that crafting open and effective communication is not merely about exchanging information; it's an art form that requires both skill and empathy.

Open communication is the lifeblood of any successful team. It instills a sense of security and allows individual members to express their thoughts without fear of judgment or repercussion. Achieving this openness doesn't happen by chance; it is a deliberate, ongoing endeavor that demands attention and active engagement from every team member.

Indeed, the cornerstone of effective communication lies in the ability to listen. Active listening, the act of being fully present while someone else speaks, involves more than just processing words. It requires an open heart and mind to truly understand the speaker's perspective. Allowing room for silence in conversations can give space for ideas and thoughts to grow and flourish.

Another fundamental aspect of honed communication is clarity. In the conveyance of ideas, precision is paramount. It eliminates ambiguity and reduces the potential for misunderstanding. Each team member should strive to articulate their points clearly and concisely, as if each word carries weight and intention behind it.

Fostering an atmosphere where feedback is not only given but invited and welcomed is a testament to effective communication within a team. Constructive criticism, offered in a spirit of support and improvement, can ignite innovation and personal growth. Team members who feel comfortable both giving and receiving feedback know their input is valued, creating a robust foundation for improvement and development.

Body language and tone also play a crucial role in communication. They are the silent undertones that can speak volumes beyond the spoken word. Being attuned to these non-verbal cues promotes a deeper understanding and connection among team members. It's a reminder that communication is not just about what is said, but also about how it's said.

Adapting one's communication style to the needs and preferences of the team is a dexterous skill. Diversity in personality and culture means there is no one-size-fits-all approach to effective dialogue. Sensitivity towards these differences can help avoid misinterpretation and build a bridge across varied communication styles.

Transparency is another integral theme in open and effective communication. It fosters trust and dissipates uncertainty, setting the stage for team members to share not only their successes but also their challenges and failures. This candidness empowers teams to face obstacles together and work collaboratively towards solutions.

Conflict is an inevitable part of any human interaction, and effective communication plays a central role in resolving these differences constructively. Rather than tiptoeing around sensitive topics, addressing them head-on in a clear, respectful manner can transform potential discord into an opportunity for team strengthening.

Delivering messages with positivity and encouragement can act like a balm, soothing any anxieties and boosting team morale. The power of positive communication lies in its ability to motivate and inspire; it's the wind beneath the wings of teamwork that propels the group to greater heights.

It's important to consider the venues and channels through which communication flows. Whether it's face-to-face meetings, emails, or virtual collaboration tools, choosing the right medium can impact the effectiveness of the message and the collaboration it seeks to foster.

Time is also a facet of communication that should not be overlooked. Regularly scheduled check-ins and updates can keep a team aligned and informed, helping to prevent the pitfalls of information silos and ensuring that everyone is moving in the right direction.

Communication, however, is not immune to the perils of excess. Overcommunication can be just as detrimental as undercommunication, leading to information overload and inefficiencies. Striking the right balance requires mindfulness and a constant pulse on the team's communication dynamics.

In fostering open and effective communication, one must acknowledge the role of vulnerability. Allowing oneself to be seen with authenticity paves the way for genuine connections and builds an environment where creativity and innovation thrive. When the team members are unafraid to show their true selves, the camaraderie and the spirit of the team reach their zenith.

The journey toward achieving open and effective communication is continuous and dynamic. It's a pivotal element in the heartbeat of teamwork, ensuring that the life-force of collaboration pulses strongly and healthily. In striving toward this goal, we can harness the tremendous power of togetherness, creating a win-win scenario for every team member involved. The rewards of such an endeavor are profound, inspiring a symphony of voices that speak in unison, driving the collective effort forward to unparalleled success.

Navigating Conflict and Building Consensus

In the pulse of teamwork, communication stands as the vital organ that ensures lifeblood flows through every facet. Within this complex system of interactions, conflicts are inevitable; they are like crescendos that challenge the harmony of a symphony. But it's not the absence of conflict that makes a team excel—it's the ability to navigate through it and build consensus that truly distinguishes it.

Understanding that conflict is often the expression of diverse perspectives and passions, we begin to see its potential to catalyze growth. It's essential to meet conflict with a mindset fixated on solutions, not strife. By harnessing the energy that comes from differing viewpoints, teams can forge pathways to innovative and inclusive resolutions.

When conflict arises, effective communication becomes more critical than ever. Active listening, a skill paramount to resolution, involves much more than hearing words—it's about understanding the message beneath them. The willingness to listen earnestly to each other creates an environment where every voice can be heard and valued.

To navigate conflict, teams must cultivate a culture of respect. Each member must trust that their concerns will be met with consideration, and that their contributions are an integral part of the tapestry of team success. Mutual respect gives rise to patience and the recognition that consensus doesn't always mean unanimous agreement, but rather a decision that the team can collectively support.

An effective strategy to cut through the complex knot of disagreements is to identify common interests. Steering the conversation away from entrenched positions toward shared goals can illuminate the avenue to consensus. Often, when common ground is acknowledged, what seemed like insurmountable differences can become mere steps along the path to a unified resolution.

However, finding this common ground requires a form of humility and vulnerability that may not come naturally in professional settings. It's about being open to the possibility that one's own perspective is not the only, or even the best, vantage point from which to see the challenge. This openness encourages a fusion of ideas, where the synthesis of collective intelligence lifts teams above the battleground of egos.

Consensus building is an art that calls for patience and iterative dialogue. It often requires compromise, and always necessitates understanding. A decision taken after thorough consideration and collaborative effort bears the hallmark of true teamwork. It's through this crucible of deliberation that a group's decision is forged with the strength to withstand future challenges.

Conflict resolution tools are myriad, but perhaps the most powerful among them is simply the manner in which team members communicate. A respectful tone, language free of accusatory or inflammatory phrases, and gestures that promote openness are all silent architects of positive outcomes.

Setting the stage for productive conflict resolution involves establishing norms for how disagreements are handled. Ground rules can ensure that conflicting parties engage with the issue, not with each other on a personal level. Defining clear processes for discussion keeps the team focused on resolution, rather than dissolution.

At times, the path to consensus requires a mediator—someone who can neutrally guide the group through the rough waters of discord. This individual must navigate with an even hand, encouraging each member to contribute and recognizing the validity in every argument. Integrity and impartiality are the compass by which they steer the team toward agreement.

Building consensus also means celebrating the small victories along the way—acknowledging when progress is made, or when a compromise is reached. These moments, though seemingly minor, are the incremental steps that lead to the peak of collective achievement.

The ultimate goal in navigating conflict and building consensus is to arrive at decisions that everyone can support and implement. A consensus that is begrudgingly accepted is fragile—it must be solid enough to sustain action and resilient enough to endure the questioning that implementation often brings.

However, it is important to recognize that not all conflict can be resolved in the moment it arises. There are times when divergent paths must be walked for a while before they converge again. In these instances, agreeing to disagree, but committing to revisit the issue, is a consensus of its own kind—it is an agreement to continue the discussion with a future-focused mindset.

In conclusion, navigating conflict and building consensus are critical competencies for a team that aspires to greatness. These are not one-time achievements but ongoing commitments to a process that values every member and their input. As teams learn to turn the cacophony of conflict into the symphony of synergy, they find themselves not just achieving goals, but transcending them.

The task ahead for any team is to see conflict not as a hindrance but as an opportunity—an opportunity for deeper understanding, for relationship building, and for crafting solutions that resonate with the collective wisdom of all its members. With each conflict navigated and consensus built, a team moves closer to the heart of what it means to truly work together.

Tools for Healthy Dispute Resolution

It's in the crucible of conflict that the strength of a team is often tested and forged. Healthy dispute resolution is not merely a skill but an indispensable tool in cultivating togetherness and ensuring that this togetherness translates into collective success.

Imagine, if you will, a team that views disagreements not as threats but as opportunities to deepen understanding and reinforce trust. Such a team harnesses a variety of tools to navigate conflict with grace and effectiveness. The first tool in the arsenal is active listening. When team members actively listen to one another, they affirm the value of each person's perspective, laying the groundwork for a resolution that respects all views.

Another essential tool is emotional intelligence—the capacity to be aware of, control, and express one's emotions judiciously and empathetically. Teams that resolve disputes effectively are adept at emotional intelligence, using it to steer conversations away from personal attacks and toward issue-based discussions. This shifts the focus from blame to collaboration in finding solutions.

Framework setting is also pivotal; it involves establishing clear guidelines for how disputes will be managed before they arise. This proactive step ensures that when tensions surface, there's a road map in place, reducing uncertainty and helping to keep discussions solution-oriented.

Moreover, joint problem-solving stands as a powerful strategy that treats conflict as a shared challenge rather than a zero-sum game. It asks individuals to step into a collaborative space, evaluating the root cause of the disagreement and brainstorming ideas that cater to the collective good rather than personal gain.

Articulation of interests is another tool that supports healthy dispute resolution. By encouraging individuals to express their underlying interests rather than positional statements, it becomes easier to uncover compatible areas and foster agreements that satisfy the core needs of the parties involved.

In addition to these tools, compromise and adaptation offer a pathway to middle ground where all parties can agree to make concessions. This doesn't mean settling for less but finding a common denominator that respects the essence of each stakeholder's perspective.

Further reinforcing these tools is the practice of patience and the avoidance of rushing to judgments. In the tapestry of teamwork, time acts as a restorative thread, allowing insights to mature and enabling individuals to approach disputes with a calmer, more considered mindset.

Lastly, post-dispute reflection is a habit that turns conflict into a learning experience. By reviewing the dispute resolution process and outcomes, teams can identify improvements for future interactions, ensuring a continual refinement of their collaborative efforts.

Incorporating these tools requires ongoing commitment and practice. Yet, the rewards are immense. Teams that excel in healthy dispute resolution not only solve problems more effectively but also reinforce their bonds, elevate their trust, and enhance their collective potential. Indeed, the true power of togetherness is found not in the absence of disagreements but in the ability to rise above them, creating win-win scenarios that echo the essence of unity and mutual success.

So as we delve into the intricacies of teamwork and collaboration, let us not shy away from the demanding but rewarding journey of mastering healthy dispute resolution. It's this mastery that propels teams from merely functioning to truly thriving, turning every tension into a triumph in the shared voyage towards greatness.

Chapter 4:
Leadership in a Collaborative World

In an era where interdependence is not just a virtue but a necessity, leadership transcends the confines of hierarchy and spreads its roots into the fertile grounds of collaboration. We've delved into the realms of teamwork and communication; now, it's time to explore how leadership evolves in this dance of mutual effort. The transformation of leadership in a collective realm capitalizes on recognizing that every individual brings a unique strength to the table. By not just allowing but fervently encouraging each team member to take the helm in their area of expertise, we foster an environment where initiative is celebrated, and accountability becomes a shared value. It's here where leaders emerge at every stratum, organically driving the team towards a vision that is not imposed but collectively owned—a vision that morphs over time with each contribution, propelling the group towards success that is both individual in achievement and unified in triumph.

Redefining Leadership for Team Success

In today's landscape of interconnected challenges and collaborative projects, leadership can no longer be confined to a single individual bearing the mantle of authority. It's about creating an environment where every team member feels empowered to take initiative and propel the collective towards success. Redefining leadership for team success is, thus, an essential discourse in the context of a collaborative world.

Leadership, in its redefined state, is more about influence than hierarchical command. A leader's primary role shifts from being the sole decision-maker to a guide who nurtures the talents and abilities of their team. It means fostering a culture where each person's contributions are not only valued but are seen as integral to the team's fabric.

Success in a team setting hinges on the ability to recognize and utilize the strengths of each member. Leaders must encourage individual team members to take ownership of their roles and understand how their unique contributions fit into the larger picture. It's about aligning personal ambitions with shared objectives to facilitate a sense of belonging and purpose.

Establishing clear communication channels forms the backbone of successful leadership in a team-centric approach. It involves not just dictating what needs to be done but, more importantly, listening to feedback and ideas from all levels of the team. This two-way dialogue instills a spirit of cooperation and ensures that everyone is on the same page.

Conflict can often arise in team dynamics, but redefined leadership turns these challenges into opportunities for growth. Through fostering an environment of respect and mutual understanding, leaders can guide teams in transforming tension into innovative solutions that benefit everyone involved.

A reimagined leader must also be adept at recognizing and celebrating the contributions of team members. It's crucial to understand that motivation and morale are strengthened when individuals are acknowledged for their efforts. This practice not only propels current projects forward but also bolsters the team for future endeavors.

Another important aspect of redefined leadership is the establishment of trust. Trust stems from consistency, vulnerability, and accountability—traits that a leader must exhibit and encourage within the team. It is the groundwork for creating a secure and open atmosphere where ideas flourish and risks are taken collaboratively.

Beyond merely managing tasks, today's leaders are mentors and coaches who prioritize the personal and professional development of their team members. They understand that the growth of individuals directly contributes to the strength and capability of the team as a whole.

To succeed in redefined leadership for team success, leaders must adapt a mindset of continuous learning. The rapidly changing world requires a commitment to stay updated with new strategies, technologies, and approaches to problem-solving.

Empathy is a cornerstone of this new leadership paradigm. Leaders must be able to put themselves in the shoes of their team members, understanding their challenges and perspectives. This emotional intelligence fosters a more cohesive and productive team dynamic.

The concept of a flat organization structure is closely tied to the redefined leadership model. It encourages a democratic approach where everyone's opinions are heard and valued, which can lead to more innovative solutions and a more invested team.

Leaders must also set the example in terms of work ethic and dedication. By showcasing their own commitment to the team's objectives and values, leaders instill a culture of dedication and high performance amongst their members.

Redefined leadership is characterized by the ability to delegate effectively. This means trusting in the abilities of team members to handle responsibilities and make decisions. It's a reflection of confidence in the team's talent and a reinforcement of their autonomy.

Ultimately, redefined leadership for team success is about cultivating an ecosystem where every member has the opportunity to become a leader in their own right. This approach is not just transformational for the individuals involved but catapults the team to greater heights of achievement and innovation.

In sum, leaders in a collaborative world must be visionaries, guides, facilitators, coaches, and champions for their team. By embracing this multi-faceted role, they can propel their teams to unprecedented success, fostering an environment where collective triumph is not just a goal, but a standard of excellence.

Cultivating Leaders at Every Level

Leadership, in its most effective form, can indeed permeate every level of an organization, creating a vibrant culture that encourages initiative and fosters growth. In a world that increasingly values collaboration, it's crucial to view leadership not as a position to be held but as a behavior to be embraced.

In a landscape marked by complexity and constant change, the traditional model of leadership—where directives flow top-down—is no longer sufficient. Instead, organizations are finding strength in cultivating leaders among all their members, an approach that makes teams more agile, adaptive, and prepared to meet challenges head-on.

Cultivating leaders at every level starts by acknowledging that each individual brings a unique perspective and a personal toolkit of skills and experiences. By recognizing the potential in everyone, we begin laying the groundwork for empowering broader leadership within the team.

Encouragement serves as a cornerstone in this cultivation process. Management must actively endorse and support every member's capacity to lead in their respective roles. Through positive reinforcement, mentorship, and recognition, members feel valued and inspired to contribute leadership of their own accord.

Opportunity is another pillar. Provide team members with opportunities to lead, regardless of their official title. It could be spearheading a project, representing the team in organizational gatherings, or leading an internal initiative—that's what equips individuals with the experience and confidence they need to grow as leaders.

An environment that endorses autonomy and trusts its members to make decisions is conducive to developing leaders. This autonomy nurtures leaders who are self-regulating, inventive, and equipped to make key decisions at critical moments, without awaiting instructions.

Knowledge sharing is also fundamental to leadership development. Through cross-training and open forums for discussion, individuals gain a more profound understanding of various aspects of the organization and are better prepared to lead when the situation calls for it.

Democratizing leadership implies a flat hierarchy where open feedback is not just welcome but expected. Communication channels should be such that ideas can flow seamlessly in all directions, empowering individuals to speak up, contribute, and effect change.

Challenges are, paradoxically, opportunities in disguise. When members face obstacles, rather than immediately seeking outside assistance, encourage them to brainstorm solutions. It's within these crucibles that leaders are forged, their problem-solving capabilities honed by the fires of necessity.

Accountability shouldn't just be a buzzword tossed around in meetings; it's a key element of leadership. Hold each team member accountable for their actions and decisions, and celebrate when they meet their objectives, reinforcing the value of responsible leadership.

Facilitating collaboration among team members is yet another way to cultivate leadership. When individuals work cohesively, they inspire each other, often stepping up to lead initiatives organically, propelling the group forward towards shared goals.

Continual learning and professional development are inherent to leadership. Offering workshops, courses, and seminars for team members to enhance their skills demonstrates a commitment to their growth and fosters a culture of continuous improvement.

Embracing diversity and inclusion in leadership development cannot be understated. A rich mosaic of leaders from various backgrounds, viewpoints, and talents enhances the collective intelligence and creativity of a team, leading to better outcomes and a more vibrant workplace culture.

In summary, cultivating leaders at every level means creating an ecosystem where each member of the organization feels empowered, responsible, and equipped to lead in their capacity. It's a journey that requires commitment, strategic vision, and an unwavering belief in the potential of every individual to contribute to the greater whole.

As we move forward, let us carry the intention to nurture leaders within us all. When people believe in their own potential and their ability to influence the collective, a powerful transformation begins. Together, we create a strong fabric of leadership that can hold the weight of any challenge and is illuminated by the light of every triumph.

Encouraging Initiative and Responsibility

In the journey of creating robust team dynamics, encouraging initiative and responsibility among team members stands as a cornerstone for cultivating leaders at every level. This is not merely an investment in individuals, but a strategic approach to building a team that is resilient, proactive, and primed for success. Emphasizing personal accountability and initiative propels teams beyond the ordinary, for when each member embraces ownership, the collective thrives.

To embolden initiative, it is imperative to foster an environment where creativity is not only welcomed but celebrated. A culture that values innovative thinking allows individuals to step outside their comfort zones. By doing so, they unlock a wellspring of potential that propels the team forward. Proactive suggestion of ideas, volunteering for new challenges, and willingness to go the extra mile become the norm when a supportive backdrop is in place.

In the same breath, responsibility is a twin pillar to initiative. Encouraging team members to take ownership of their work involves trusting them to make decisions and giving them the autonomy to see projects through. This sense of responsibility strengthens their commitment to the team's shared goals, fostering a deeper connection to the team's success. It also lays the groundwork for accountability, a crucial component for maintaining high performance standards.

Setting clear expectations is a critical step in promoting responsibility. When members are aware of what is required of them, including the quality of work and timelines, it instills a professional discipline that is invaluable. Concurrently, providing the necessary resources and support empowers them to meet these expectations with a sense of purpose and self-assuredness.

Recognition plays a vital role in sustaining initiative and responsibility. Acknowledging individual contributions fortifies their sense of belonging and worth within the team. This recognition becomes a powerful motivator, propelling members to continue taking initiative and embracing responsibility with zeal.

To ensure that the seeds of initiative and responsibility germinate, it is essential for leadership to exemplify these qualities. Leaders must portray the very behaviors they wish to nurture in their teams. By walking the talk, they become the embodiment of the team's values, inspiring members through their actions.

Mentorship is another tool through which initiative and responsibility can be cultivated. Pairing seasoned team members with newer ones not only enables the transfer of skills but also instills confidence. Through this guided autonomy, emerging team players can navigate their way, learning to take initiative and be accountable for their contributions in a supportive environment.

Open dialogue and constructive feedback are the foundations upon which initiative and responsibility are encouraged. They allow for the reflection necessary to understand what practices serve the team's objectives and which do not. Encouraging team members to share their thoughts and experiences promotes a culture where everyone has a voice and a stake in the team's direction and achievements.

Finally, embracing failures as learning opportunities is central to fostering these qualities. When team members understand that setbacks are not deterrents but stepping stones for growth, they become more inclined to take calculated risks. This environment of psychological safety supports the exploration and testing of new ideas, which is the lifeblood of innovation and improvement.

By embedding the values of initiative and responsibility into the DNA of team culture, you lay a sturdy foundation for a group that not only achieves but excels. It creates a cycle of empowerment and success where every member knows that their contributions are meaningful and that they hold the power to effect change, leading to the power of togetherness and the creation of win-win scenarios for everyone involved.

Chapter 5:
Leveraging Diversity for Innovative Outcomes

As we pivot from the influential dynamics of leadership, we find ourselves at the heart of ingenuity—diversity. It's not just a buzzword; it's the crucible in which the most groundbreaking ideas are forged. Diversity is the wellspring of creativity from which teams can drink to quench their thirst for innovation. By embracing the unique backgrounds, experiences, and thought processes each team member brings to the table, we set the stage for breakthroughs that could never be achieved in homogenous environments. In this chapter, we examine how we can create the conditions necessary to translate individual differences into collective assets. It's an artful balance—cultivating an inclusive culture where every voice can resonate with its own timbre, yet harmonize within the broader symphony of teamwork. Here, we explore the strategies to harness these diverse talents, ensuring they're not just present but are powerfully contributing to innovation that pushes the bounds of what's possible, paving the way for transformative outcomes that benefit all.

The Power of Different Perspectives

In our journey together through the intricacies of teamwork, we have explored the bedrock of collaboration, the unifying force of shared goals, and the rhythm of effective communication. As we delve deeper into the enriching soil of collaborative efforts, we discover a gem that is often overlooked yet invaluable: the power of different perspectives.

When harnessed correctly, varying viewpoints can become the alchemy that transforms a group of individuals into a crucible for innovation. Teams that embrace a multitude of perspectives are not merely cooperating; they are co-creating a tapestry of thought that is rich with diverse strands of insight and experience.

Imagine you are in a room filled with minds from different cultures, professions, and backgrounds. Each person is a living library, teeming with chapters of unique experiences. Now consider the potency of decision-making within this room. Each individual's view is a refraction of the world, a kaleidoscope through which problems can be dissected and ideas can flourish in multidimensional ways.

This extraordinary blend of perspectives nurtures innovation as each unique angle provides a distinct approach to problem-solving. As the Chinese proverb says, "When there is light in the soul, there is beauty in the person; when there is beauty in the person, there is harmony in the house; when there is harmony in the house, there is order in the nation; when there is order in the nation, there is peace in the world."

Similarly, when there is light in the form of diverse perspectives within a team, there is beauty in the solutions created; when there is beauty in the solutions, there is harmony in the organization; and with harmony in the organization, there is the potential for a significant impact on the world beyond its walls.

The brilliance of different perspectives is not just in the variety of ideas presented but in the dynamic interactions that arise. These interactions often lead to a fusion of concepts, creating outcomes that are more robust and comprehensive than any single perspective could offer.

It is pivotal, however, to distinguish mere diversity of opinion from the true integration of different perspectives. The former can lead to discord if not managed with skill, while the latter requires a culture that not only allows but also encourages multiple viewpoints to engage in a dialogue that is respectful, open, and constructive.

To facilitate this, leaders must become the architects of forums where such exchange is possible. They must design an environment that acts as a crucible for these elements to come together safely, where the sometimes volatile reactions of contrasting ideas can be tempered and guided to a constructive synthesis.

One must also consider the frame of mind required to effectively leverage these perspectives. It necessitates humility to recognize that no single individual has all the answers, and it demands curiosity to seek understanding and value in the unexplored territory of another's viewpoint.

Additionally, there is a need for courage to venture into the unfamiliar, to question the status quo, and to challenge the group's collective assumptions. It is from the fertile soil of this discomfort that new solutions sprout and thrive.

Leveraging different perspectives also implies an intricate balance between conviction and flexibility. While one must have the confidence to voice and defend a unique point of view, it is just as imperative to possess the agility to adapt and realign when presented with compelling alternative insights.

In practice, the confluence of different perspectives can lead to a phenomenon known as creative abrasion. This process is not unlike the geological formation of diamonds, where carbon must endure immense pressure to transform into a priceless jewel. Similarly, a team's ideas must withstand the pressure of debate and scrutiny to crystallize into innovation.

The beauty of diversity in thought is not just about the creation of better products, services, or strategies – it's about building a vibrant workplace where each individual feels valued and known. When people believe their perspectives matter, they are more engaged, more invested, and indisputably more productive.

The narrative of history is replete with examples where a singular shift in perspective has led to groundbreaking discoveries. It behooves us, then, to foster a culture that not only permits but pursues the inclusion of diverse perspectives, for it is within this kaleidoscope that the solutions to our greatest challenges are waiting to be found.

In the subsequent chapters, we will dive further into creating inclusive environments and strategies to harness diverse talents effectively. Yet, it is the power of different perspectives that remains a central theme resonating through the collective wisdom of any successful team. By valuing this diversity of thought, we set the stage for unforeseen innovation and a robust path toward achieving truly transformative outcomes.

Creating Inclusive Environments

In an age where diversity has become the tapestry of the modern workplace, inclusive environments are not just an ideal, they are imperative for innovation and success. Embracing the myriad of experiences, perspectives, and skills that each individual brings to the table, fosters the kind of creativity and dynamism that can turn ordinary outcomes into extraordinary ones.

Creating an inclusive environment begins with recognition – recognizing that each person has value beyond the sum of their skills. It's about looking past superficial differences and drilling into the core of what makes each person unique. This does not mean merely tolerating differences, but actively seeking them out and celebrating them.

However, recognizing diversity's worth is only the first step. Inclusion involves integrating this awareness into every facet of team operations. It's about constructing systems and processes that accommodate diverse needs and preferences and that invite contributions from all members.

To leverage true diversity, teams must establish ground rules that foster open-mindedness. Listening to one another with the intent to understand rather than the intent to reply, breaks down barriers and uncovers insights that might otherwise be missed. It is through the collective synthesis of diverse ideas that innovative solutions are born.

It's also critical that leadership plays an influential role in fostering inclusiveness. When leaders model inclusive behaviors – when they ask questions, engage in active listening, and promote an atmosphere of respect – they set the tone for the entire organization.

Yet, beyond policies and leadership initiatives, the soul of inclusiveness lies within each team member's daily interactions. Every person has the responsibility to cultivate a warm environment where colleagues feel comfortable expressing themselves without the fear of judgment or reprisal.

Inclusive environments are safe environments. Team members must feel secure in taking risks and making mistakes without fear of adverse consequences. Psychological safety is the bedrock of high-performing teams, paving the way for the confidence to innovate and push boundaries.

Moreover, an inclusive environment recognizes and incorporates different working and learning styles. Not every team member will shine in a boisterous brainstorming session, just as some may struggle with silent reflection. Providing multiple avenues for contribution ensures that all voices are heard and valued.

As teams work toward inclusiveness, training plays a crucial role. Training initiatives that provide skills in cross-cultural communication, unconscious bias awareness, and conflict resolution are fundamental to building the skill set necessary for managing diversity.

It's essential to understand that inclusion is an ongoing journey, not a destination. As our understanding of diversity deepens and the demographic make-up of teams changes, the strategies for inclusion will evolve. Teams must be committed to regular reflection and adaptation to remain at the forefront of inclusive practice.

Inculcating an ethos of inclusion also means recognizing and rewarding those behaviors that promote diversity. When the team sees inclusion as part of the path to personal success, it reinforces the importance and value of such behaviors every day.

An inclusive environment is also a fair environment. When fairness is the norm, trust grows, and when trust grows, people are more willing to be vulnerable and authentic – key to innovative team dynamics. Equity in opportunity and the assurance that every member's contributions are valued equally encourage a deeper investment from the team.

Ultimately, creating inclusive environments is about harnessing the power of humanity's full spectrum of talent. It's not merely a matter of ethics but of practicality. The richest solutions and most profound advances come from the collision of different ideas, the melding of perspectives, and the synergy that can only be achieved through genuine inclusivity.

Teams that master the art of creating inclusive environments can expect a transformation. As they embrace the strengths that lie in their diversity, they will experience a positive shift in team dynamics, output, and overall team satisfaction. A culture of inclusion does not materialize overnight, but with commitment and diligence, the efforts will resonate throughout every outcome, driving innovation and success to new heights.

In conclusion, remember that inclusive environments are about valuing every individual's unique contributions while fostering a sense of belongingness and equity. With the foundational understanding that together, our collective capabilities far exceed our individual limitations, creating and maintaining an atmosphere of inclusion is the most certain path to achieving truly innovative and transformative outcomes.

Strategies for Harnessing Diverse Talents

Within a collective endeavor, the strategic harnessing of diverse talents is not just recommended; it's imperative for crafting innovative outcomes and achieving unity in vision. The question then becomes, how can one effectively bring together the various skills, backgrounds, and personalities each team member offers? It is within the response to this question that the potential for a remarkable synergy lies.

At the core of this approach is the appreciation of diversity beyond surface-level acknowledgments. By embracing the idea that each person's experiences and ways of thinking contribute unique value, we begin to see diversity as a catalyzing force. It's critical for team leaders and members alike to create spaces where open dialogue about diverse perspectives is encouraged and facilitated with respect and genuine curiosity.

Integral to this conversation is the need to set aside assumptions and embrace a learner's mindset. Rather than being constrained by the "way we've always done it," consider how combining different talents can lead to a new set of best practices. These emerging practices could better align with the evolving landscape of your collective objectives and the changing dynamics of your team.

Of course, recognizing talent is one thing; leveraging it practically is another. Therefore, it's essential to conduct an analysis of your team's strengths and weaknesses through various lenses. This involves not just evaluating technical skills but also considering interpersonal dynamics, emotional intelligence, and problem-solving abilities. A team with a rich tapestry of complementary strengths will position itself well for tackling complex challenges.

From this analysis, goal alignment is key. All team members should understand how their distinct roles and the talents they bring contribute to shared objectives. It's empowering for individuals to see a direct line from their contributions to team successes. Goal alignment underscores the value of every team member and increases overall commitment and cohesion.

Encouraging a culture of mentorship and knowledge-sharing across different areas of expertise further strengthens talent utilization. More seasoned team members can offer guidance, while new members can bring fresh perspectives and innovative ideas. This reciprocal teaching and learning solidify a foundation for continual growth and adaptation.

Moreover, innovative problem-solving sessions, such as hackathons and brainstorming workshops, can be leveraged to break conventional thought patterns. They create a playground for diverse talents to intersect, combining varied insights and generating unorthodox solutions that could revolutionize approaches to everyday challenges.

Recognition plays a nontrivial role in sustaining motivation and validating the diverse contributions of team members. Celebrate not only the outcomes but also the creative thinking and collaborative efforts that made them possible. Recognition reinforces positive behaviors and further incentivizes team members to offer their unique capabilities to group endeavors.

Creating opportunities for leadership at every level ensures that diverse talents are not only acknowledged but are also given the power to lead changes and drive initiatives. Such opportunities invigorate team members and encourage them to invest more deeply in collective goals. It's crucial for everyone to believe that they can make a real difference within the team construct.

To conclude, harnessing diverse talents requires thoughtful strategies, responsive leadership, and a culture that thrives on mutual respect and continuous learning. These elements combine to create a dynamic ecosystem wherein every individual feels valued, and their unique abilities are effectively synchronized towards common goals. In doing so, we don't just assemble a team; we forge a powerful alliance capable of reaching unprecedented heights.

Chapter 6:
Trust: The Glue of Teamwork

Trust forms the bedrock upon which the edifice of effective teamwork is built. It is the binding agent that allows individuals to act as a single, cohesive unit, propelling the team towards the realization of a shared vision. Within the sanctuary of trust, team members openly share their vulnerabilities, confident in the knowledge that their contributions and concerns are valued and respected. This foundation of trust does not emerge spontaneously but grows from the seeds of consistency, reliability, and integrity planted by each individual. When trust prevails, accountability becomes a shared endeavour, and the fear of failure diminishes, as the team understands that setbacks are collective learning experiences from which they will emerge stronger. The essence of trust is the understanding that the strengths of the team are fortified by each member, and that its solidity is contingent upon the unwavering support members provide to one another. Nurturing this sacred bond within the team transforms not only the group's dynamic but also magnifies the potential for incredible achievements.

Building and Maintaining Trust

In the grand tapestry of teamwork, trust is the thread that binds individual members into a robust fabric. It's the firm foundation upon which the mighty edifice of collaboration is built, and without it, even the most skilled groups can crumble. The quest to build and maintain trust within a team is a continuous journey that demands careful attention and consistent effort, for trust is as delicate as it is crucial.

Building trust starts with authenticity. To be seen as trustworthy, a leader or a team member must be genuine in their interactions. People trust those who present themselves honestly, flaws and all, rather than those who seem to be playing a part. This authenticity fosters a sense of reliability, as team members come to believe that what they see is what they get. In this ambiance of authenticity, trust flourishes.

Open communication is another vital element in the trust-building process. It involves not only the straightforward exchange of ideas but also the willingness to engage in challenging conversations. When team members feel their voices are heard and valued, a deep sense of trust begins to permeate the team. Furthermore, when leaders demonstrate transparent decision-making processes, team members are more likely to extend their trust even during times of uncertainty.

Consistency in words and actions reinforces trust. When people follow through on their commitments and uphold their promises, it signals reliability. A pattern of consistency shows the team that each member is dependable and in this reliability, a powerful bond of trust is anchored.

Trust doesn't end with reliability; it also hinges on competence. Team members who consistently demonstrate their capability in their roles inspire a sense of confidence in their abilities. As every member showcases their expertise, the collective trust in each other's abilities to perform tasks and solve problems. It's this belief in each individual's capacity that underpins the team's overall performance.

Another cornerstone in the edifice of trust is respect. Recognizing and valuing the inherent worth and potential of each member cultivates a culture of esteem. When individuals feel respected, they are more inclined to reciprocate trust because a mutual understanding of each member's value is recognized and acknowledged.

Forgiveness is also integral to maintaining trust. In every team's life cycle, mistakes are made. However, when errors are met with a willingness to understand, learn, and move forward, rather than with punitive measures, trust is reinforced. It sends a clear message that the team is a safe place to take risks and grow, a concept crucial for innovation and continuous improvement.

Empathy goes hand in hand with forgiveness as a trust-building tool. Understanding the perspectives and feelings of team members creates emotional connections that tie the fabric of trust tighter. An empathetic approach by everyone within the team paves the way for stronger, more trustworthy relationships.

Accountability is equally instrumental in nurturing trust. When individuals take responsibility for their actions and are held accountable for their roles, it strengthens the team's trust in one another. It solidifies the belief that every member will uphold their part of the team's shared journey towards success.

In the same vein, recognition of each other's contributions bolsters trust. Acknowledging and celebrating the accomplishments of team members not only motivates but also reinforces the trust that each person's efforts are valued and impactful.

Challenging yet supportive environments are fundamental to maintaining trust. Although high expectations are set, providing the needed support to meet these expectations reassures team members that they are not alone in their endeavors. It is this balance of challenge and support that fortifies the trust among team members.

This web of trust woven within a team is not static; it requires continuous nurturing. The momentum of building trust is maintained through regular team-building activities, retreats, and open forums for discussion. These repeated interactions remind everyone of the shared journey they are on and the mutual trust required to navigate it.

Change is inevitable, and when it comes, maintaining trust requires adaptability and open-mindedness. Teams that trust are better equipped to navigate the shifting sands of their environment because they are bound by a shared belief in their collective strength and adaptability.

Inculcating a commitment to growth and learning also ensures the longevity of trust. As team members strive to be better and learn together, they not only build trust in each other but also establish a culture of continuous improvement. Learning from setbacks instead of allowing them to sow seeds of distrust becomes a reflex founded on the strong belief in the team's resilience.

Lastly, trust is built through shared experiences and memories. The trials and triumphs endured together solidify the trust built within a team. These shared experiences become the narrative of the team's journey, a tale of trust that grows stronger with each challenge and success.

In closing, building and maintaining trust is an ongoing narrative of sincerity, communication, reliability, competence, respect, forgiveness, empathy, accountability, recognition, support, activity, adaptability, learning, and shared experiences. Trust is not merely the glue of teamwork; it is the cornerstone of an edifice where collective success is built on the strength of each trusted member. It is this ethos of trust that transforms a group of individuals into an indomitable team, and it's this spirit of unity that turns individual success into a harmonized triumph.

Vulnerability and Accountability in Teams

It's often said that the strength of a chain lies in its weakest link, and this metaphor extends seamlessly into the fabric of teamwork. Values such as trust and transparency are foundational, yet their potency is significantly enhanced by a team's ability to embrace vulnerability and accountability. Delving into this realm provides a profound opportunity for transformation, not only for individuals but for the collective as a whole.

To understand the role of vulnerability in a team, one must recognize that it is the birthplace of innovation, creativity, and change. It involves the courage to be open about one's thoughts, challenges, and mistakes. When individuals feel safe enough to be vulnerable, they are more likely to share diverse ideas and perspectives, leading to richer collaboration and more robust solutions.

Accountability goes hand-in-hand with vulnerability. It means taking responsibility for one's actions and contributions to the team. Accountability isn't just about admitting to errors; it's also about owning one's part of the team effort, regardless of the outcome. When each team member upholds this standard, trust deepens, creating a bedrock for sustained collective success.

In a culture that prizes vulnerability, leaders must lead by example. The willingness of those at the helm to show their own imperfections sets a precedent. It becomes clear that the team's value does not rest solely on being infallible but on the capacity to learn, adapt, and grow from every situation.

Yet, for vulnerability to truly be a transformative force, it needs the right environment—one that cultivates safety and belonging. This environment must assure members that their risks in sharing will not be met with retribution or ridicule, but with support and understanding. Only in this setting can the seeds of genuine communication and powerful collaboration take root.

However, nurturing such an environment requires more than mere intention. It demands consistent and refined processes that encourage and reward vulnerability and accountability. These processes include regular check-ins, transparent goal-setting, feedback loops, and clear expectations for every member's role and deliverables.

Accountability in a team setting also involves clarity in measuring performance. Leaders must establish and communicate specific metrics and outcomes against which team performance is gauged. These metrics must align with the team's vision and goals, providing a compass for individual contributions and group achievements.

Feedback is another crucial component in this equation. Constructive, timely, and honest feedback can reinforce accountability while also providing the necessary insights for improvement. When feedback is delivered with respect and empathy, it reinforces the culture of mutual growth and continuous learning.

Nevertheless, accountability can become a double-edged sword when mishandled. It should never devolve into a blame game. The focus must remain on progress and solutions rather than dwelling on mistakes. When challenges arise, the team should come together to strategize on steps forward, rather than dividing and pointing fingers.

Ideally, rewards and recognition should be aligned with accountable behaviors. Celebrating small victories when team members effectively demonstrate accountability can inspire others to follow suit. These celebrations can take many forms but should always reinforce the team's values and goals.

Moreover, the process of holding one another accountable can foster autonomy and empowerment. When individuals take charge of their roles and the outcomes attached to them, they are more invested in the team's success. Empowerment in this sense isn't merely about authority; it's about trust and the responsibility that comes with it.

When vulnerability and accountability are present, conflict becomes a powerful tool rather than a disruptive force. Through the lens of these values, disagreements are transformed into opportunities for deeper understanding and problem-solving. This perspective shift is essential for converting potentially harmful tensions into growth and innovation.

Vulnerability also invites empathy, a vital component of effective teamwork. When team members can put themselves in another's shoes, the dynamic shifts from judgment to support. This empathy is a catalyst for stronger relationships and more cohesive teams that can withstand and overcome any adversities.

In conclusion, vulnerability and accountability are the lifelines that sustain and fortify the trust within a team. When these facets are integrated into the team's culture, they unlock potential and drive performance to unparalleled heights. The courage to be vulnerable and the integrity to be accountable may indeed require a leap of faith, but the outcomes are worth the leap - stronger bonds, unwavering trust, and collective success beyond imagination.

Building a team where vulnerability and accountability are cornerstone principles may present challenges, but the rewards are indisputable. It lays the groundwork for an atmosphere where every individual doesn't just feel like part of a team—they feel like part of a team that is unstoppable. And when a team feels unstoppable, the limits of what they can achieve together stretch into horizons yet unseen.

Cultivating Safety and Belonging is intrinsic to the fabric of any successful team. When individuals feel safe and like they belong, the full potential of their unique contributions can be unleashed, leading to greater innovation, productivity, and satisfaction within a team. This sense of security is not merely the absence of fear. It is a proactive nurturing of an environment where everyone can share their thoughts without harsh judgment, can learn without undue embarrassment of making mistakes, and can confidently contribute to the collective goals.

In a world where competition often takes precedence, it's easy to overlook the importance of fostering these principles. Yet it is in the nurturing soil of safety and belonging that trust takes root and grows. Developing a team atmosphere where every member can voice their opinions and doubts allows for deeper connections, understanding, and shared responsibility. Team members become invested not only in their work but in each other's growth and success.

Building a sense of belonging is not about assimilation, but rather about celebrating individuality within a collective framework. The richness of diverse backgrounds, perspectives, and skills is what, in fact, propels a team toward exciting and uncharted terrains of innovation. Acknowledging and honoring each person's unique identity within a team amplifies this sense of belonging and reinforces the team's identity as a whole.

We must encourage teams to establish shared customs and traditions that celebrate the team's identity and achievements. These shared experiences act as the mortar, binding each unique brick to create a stronghold of solidarity. Traditions — whether they are regular team lunches, annual retreats, or simple morning huddles — help reinforce the shared vision and goals, and in turn, each member's role in achieving them.

Communication, too, plays a formidable role in cultivating safety and belonging. It must be transparent, consistent, and imbued with empathy. It's essential to establish and maintain open lines of discourse, listening attentively, and providing support where needed. Members should feel not just permitted but encouraged to speak up, ask for help, or offer constructive feedback.

Leadership within the team must understand that psychological safety doesn't sprout overnight; it requires constant care and reaffirmation. Leaders must exemplify and articulate the behaviors that foster an inclusive environment – listening attentively, acknowledging the good, and offering support during challenges. By spotlighting members' strengths and demonstrating appreciation for their uniqueness, leaders can also fortify the sense of belonging among team members.

This sense of safety and belonging isn't limited to the confines of team interactions. It should be evident in how the team rallies around a colleague facing personal setbacks or celebrates significant milestones in each other's lives. This expression of genuine care and connection elevates a group from being just a team to being a community.

In an era where remote work and digital communication are common, the concept of a team transcends physical space. This makes it even more crucial to implement intentional practices that bridge gaps and create a cohesive virtual community. Regular check-ins, virtual team-building activities, and digital platforms for celebrating accomplishments can all contribute to maintaining this vital bond.

Ultimately, cultivating safety and belonging leads to the empowerment of each member. When team members feel secure, they are more inclined to go beyond their roles, to innovate, to take calculated risks, and to stay true to their authentic selves. This is the foundation upon which extraordinary teams are built, and on which they thrive — not just within the immediate team boundaries, but as a beacon of potential for every team they interact with.

A team that succeeds in creating this kind of environment coalesces around the undeniable power of togetherness, making every victory sweeter because it's shared with others who value one another's welfare as much as their own success. Cultivating safety and belonging, therefore, isn't just beneficial. It's the cornerstone of team excellence, where collective triumph weaves through the fabric of individual achievements, creating a tapestry of success that is as resilient as it is beautiful.

Chapter 7:
Motivation and Commitment in Teams

In the journey toward collective mastery, Chapter 7 delves into the catalysts of group dynamism—motivation and commitment. It's vital that we understand what drives each member to rise within their team, recognizing that the source of this energy may stem from both intrinsic desires and extrinsic rewards. Core to the spirit of any successful team is how these motivators are harnessed to instill a deep-seated sense of dedication and camaraderie. Leaders and teammates alike must become artisans in crafting an environment where motivation flourishes, recognizing efforts genuinely and celebrating collective victories with zeal. This chapter isn't just about engendering commitment but about elevating it to reflect a shared passion for achieving common objectives where every win is a stepping stone towards greater team spirit.

Understanding Intrinsic and Extrinsic Motivators

In the realm of collaborative effort and unified labor, the propulsion that drives individuals towards excellence often stems from a complex interplay of internal and external forces. These forces, known as intrinsic and extrinsic motivators, serve as the backbone to the principles that ignite the spirit of commitment and energy within team environments. To truly harness the power of togetherness, one must possess a deep understanding of these motivators and how they can be leveraged to foster an atmosphere of mutual support and shared success.

Intrinsic motivation is the internal desire to perform a task for the satisfaction and challenge it provides, rather than for some external reward. It's the spark inside each person that cries out for mastery, autonomy, and purpose. When individuals engage in work that aligns with their values and passions, the flame of intrinsic motivation burns bright, driving them to contribute their best efforts naturally and enthusiastically.

Consider, for instance, the artist whose brush strokes are guided by a deep well of creative passion, or the scientist whose quest for knowledge transcends worldly accolades. In a team setting, when each member is engaged in roles they intrinsically enjoy, the collective output is not just amplified; it is enriched with genuine fervor and care.

On the other side of the motivational spectrum lies extrinsic motivation, which is influenced by external factors such as rewards, recognition, and consequences. It's the carrot and the stick, the applause from the crowd, the bonuses and the accolades that often come with achieving certain benchmarks. These motivators are not to be underestimated, for they can emerge as powerful drivers of behavior, encouraging team members to push through challenges and perform at their best.

However, while extrinsic motivators can have a significant impact, they possess a duality in their nature. An overreliance on external rewards can potentially undermine intrinsic motivation, leading to a decline in engagement over time if not balanced carefully. As such, the efficacy of extrinsic motivators can be seen as a short-term catalyst rather than a standalone solution for fostering long-term commitment.

The art of motivation in teams, therefore, lies in balancing these two forces—to kindle the intrinsic passion within team members while strategically utilizing extrinsic rewards to maintain motivation and focus on the tasks at hand. Leaders who understand this dynamic can create environments where each motivator complements the other, leading to a more vibrant and committed team culture.

Imagine a team where each individual is working on projects that align with their interests and strengths while also being recognized and rewarded for their collective achievements. This equilibrium creates a symphony of motivation that reverberates through the entire team, driving productivity and commitment to new heights.

In an era where individualism and personal gain are often celebrated, the true essence of team success lies in our capacity to find common ground, to seek out that which propels us forward, together. When team members see the value of their contributions resonating beyond their personal gain, a shared vision comes to life, and collective goals become attainable.

To implement this understanding of motivators effectively, leaders must devote time to know their team members on a deeper level. They must uncover what sparks joy and engagement in each person and structure roles and responsibilities around these insights. By doing so, they cultivate a fertile ground for intrinsic motivation to flourish.

Similarly, extrinsic rewards should be carefully designed to not only recognize individual achievement but also to celebrate collaborative milestones. By tying recognition to team objectives and shared victories, leaders can simultaneously validate the individual effort and reinforce the collective identity of the team.

It's also essential to ensure that the extrinsic motivators provided are perceived as fair and equitable by all team members. Any sense of favoritism or inequity can erode trust and dampen the motivational climate within the team. Therefore, transparency and consistency in the distribution of rewards can help sustain high levels of extrinsic motivation.

Challenges arise when intrinsic and extrinsic motivators are out of alignment. A team leader must be vigilant in identifying signs of motivational imbalance—such as diminishing enthusiasm, complacency, or a fixation on rewards—and address them through open dialogue and strategic adjustments. This might mean realigning tasks with individual passions or refining the rewards system to better suit team values.

When both intrinsic and extrinsic motivators are woven together in the tapestry of teamwork, they enable individuals and teams to transcend the ordinary. They evolve to embody a whole that is truly greater than the sum of its parts, a tapestry that is both resilient and radiant, capable of facing the challenges of the present while reaching towards the shared dreams of the future.

As we delve into the heart of motivation and commitment in teams, let us acknowledge and respect the dual nature of what drives us. It is through this recognition and understanding that we can unlock the full potential of our collective endeavors, creating a win-win scenario for everyone involved—a scenario where achievements are celebrated, bonds are strengthened, and the power of togetherness is realized in its most profound expression.

Fostering Dedication and Team Spirit

Dedication and team spirit are the lifeblood of any thriving team. They're the qualities that can propel a group of individuals to perform at their highest potential, creating a force far stronger than the sum of its parts. To cultivate these qualities, it begins with a shared commitment to a common purpose. The most cohesive teams are bound by a powerful alliance to not only achieve their goals but to elevate each member in the quest to do so.

Such a commitment can't be forced; it must be fostered. This happens when each team member sees the vision of what can be achieved and feels a genuine stake in the outcome. They understand that their individual contributions are valued and that their personal growth is integral to the team's success. When this alignment is in place, dedication naturally flows.

Team spirit, however, requires an additional layer. It sprouts from the camaraderie that develops as a group faces challenges, celebrates successes, and shares the weight of setbacks together. To nurture this spirit, it's crucial to foster an environment where members cheer for each other, recognize one another's strengths and step in to uplift each other during tough times.

Great team spirit is also cultivated through shared experiences. These can range from work-related achievements to social gatherings or community service projects. Such activities reinforce the bonds of the team and create a reservoir of goodwill that members can draw upon when work gets challenging.

Despite the effort to build an unshakeable team spirit, even the most dedicated teams can lose their spark. Recognizing and intervening in these moments is essential. Leaders and team members alike must remain vigilant, ready to reignite the flames of enthusiasm and remind themselves why their work matters.

Another aspect of fostering dedication lies in creating a culture of consistent improvement. The best teams possess an insatiable desire to push beyond their limits, not just for the sake of personal accolades but for the advancement of the whole team. This culture is cultivated by setting progressive goals and valuing learning from every outcome, win or lose.

Communication is another cornerstone of team spirit. Open dialogues about aspirations, the direction of the team, and the challenges they're facing can make all the difference between a disconnected group and a unified force. It's through communication that trust is built, a trust which forms an unspoken pact among team members to hold each other's ambitions as sacred as their own.

To foster such dedication, roles and responsibilities must be clearly defined and aligned with team objectives. When members understand their place in the bigger picture, they're more likely to pour heart and soul into their tasks. Ownership and a sense of personal investment naturally follow.

Leaders must also lead by example in demonstrating dedication and team spirit. When those at the helm show a relentless commitment to the team's objectives and the well-being of its members, it sets a powerful example. They must celebrate not just the accomplishments, but the qualities that contributed to them: teamwork, perseverance, and mutual support.

Recognition is another powerful tool in fostering dedication. When individuals and the team as a whole are recognized for their commitment, it validates their efforts and fuels their desire to continue pushing forward. This recognition can take many forms, from public acknowledgments to development opportunities.

Moreover, fostering dedication and spirit requires patience. Teams might falter in their sense of purpose or togetherness at times, but during such periods, it's crucial to remain steadfast, listening and understanding, gently steering them back to the heart of their collective pursuit. It is often in these valleys that the deepest sense of team spirit is forged.

Creating rituals can also instill a strong sense of unity and purpose within the team. Whether it's a morning huddle to set the day's intention, regular check-ins, or a special way to sign off on a successful project, rituals remind team members of their shared experiences and the team culture they have built.

The physical workspace can also impact dedication and team spirit. Spaces that facilitate collaboration, encourage openness, and spark creativity can make team members feel more connected to each other and their joint mission.

In conclusion, dedication and team spirit don't appear overnight. They're the outcome of mindful cultivation - a garden that requires constant care. Through commitment to shared goals, open communication, recognition, and a collective culture of continual growth, teams can lift themselves to heights unattainable by any single member venturing alone. It's in the fertile soil of togetherness that success takes root, blossoms, and thrives.

As like minds join forces, driven by a deep-seated dedication to the vision they share, the spirit of the team becomes unshakeable. This unity, this inextinguishable team spirit, becomes the beacon that guides each member and the team as a whole through the complexities of collaboration towards the iridescent horizon of collective triumph.

Recognizing Efforts and Celebrating Wins is a vital component in the sphere of teamwork and collaboration. When individuals come together to achieve a shared goal, each member's contribution is a strand woven into the broader tapestry of success. In acknowledging efforts and rejoicing in collective victories, teams engender a sense of accomplishment and propel members towards ongoing commitment.

The acknowledgement of each individual's effort, regardless of the magnitude of success, is essential to cultivating an environment where members feel valued. It is in the genuine expression of gratitude for the small steps, the perseverance through challenges, and the dedication to the team's vision, that a culture of appreciation is fostered. When people feel recognized, their motivation to contribute meaningfully and to invest themselves in the team's aspirations is heightened. This notable acknowledgment often leads to an increase in individual productivity, which in turn benefits the entity as a whole.

Celebrating wins, be they minor milestones or major triumphs, serves as a reinforcement of the team's capabilities. It affirms the belief that together, as a united front, any obstacle can be surmounted and any summit can be reached. These celebrations can take many forms, from formal gatherings to informal commendations, but what is fundamental is that these moments of joy are shared and experienced by all members of the team. Celebratory practices should align with the team's values and encourage a spirit of togetherness.

Festivities and accolades should also be inclusive to ensure that no contribution is deemed too small. A team's victory is the sum of all its parts, and in recognizing the diversity of contributions, from the spearheaders to the supporters, inclusivity remains central. This reinforces mutual respect and enhances team unity, which is paramount for any group aiming for continued success.

Yet, it is critical to strike a balance, ensuring that recognition and celebrations do not foster complacency, but rather embolden the team to set higher standards and pursue greater objectives. These acknowledgments should act as stepping stones, leading to an ethos of continuous improvement and unyielding ambition. The collective pride garnered from wins should translate into a dynamic vigor that propels the team forward.

Furthermore, the manner in which teams recognize efforts and celebrate successes can serve as a reflection of their overall ethos and operational principles. Transparent and equitable recognition can strengthen trust within the team, making clear that fairness and meritocracy are not just spoken values, but ones that are actively upheld. This, in turn, champions the principle that every member's input is indispensable to the shared vision.

In recognizing efforts, creative and personalized approaches speak volumes about the team's investment in its members. Whether through personalized acknowledgments, public acclamations, or professional development opportunities, the methods employed should resonate with the individuals and underscore their unique value to the team.

It is also imperative for celebrations to underscore the linkage between individual achievements and the overarching team objectives. This helps validate the collaborative strategy at play and emphasizes the importance of unity in diversity. By doing so, it becomes apparent that while individual brilliance is commendable, it is the collective harnessing of these skills that leads to extraordinary outcomes.

In conclusion, recognizing efforts and celebrating wins is not merely a pleasant add-on to team life; it is a strategic imperative that fuels a positive cycle of performance and satisfaction. By weaving acknowledgment throughout the fabric of team operations, a sense of belonging and a hunger for continued excellence takes root. This powerful dynamic leads to the realization that together, not only can teams achieve more, but they can also elevate the experience of achievement to new heights.

Celebrate each victory, learn from every challenge, and consistently affirm the individual strengths that each member brings to the collective table. In doing so, the bond of collaboration is reinforced, ambitions soar, and the power of togetherness becomes not just an ideal, but a tangible driving force toward greater success.

Chapter 8:
Team Adaptability and Resilience

In an ever-changing landscape, the hallmark of a triumphant team is not just in its ability to execute strategies efficiently, but also in its capacity to endure and evolve amid adversity. Chapter 8 delves into the core attributes of adaptability and resilience that empower groups to not just survive, but to thrive when faced with inevitable shifts and challenges. Our journey through previous chapters has fortified the groundwork of collaboration, trust, and motivation; now we pivot to mastering the art of embracing change fearlessly. It's about cultivating a culture where flexibility is intertwined with a learning mindset, readying each member to pivot with poise and harness unforeseen obstacles as stepping stones to innovation. The capacity of a team to stand firm, learn from setbacks, and advance with renewed vigor is what sets apart the good from the great, ensuring that each wave of transformation is ridden with finesse and foresight.

Embracing Change as a Constant

In the tapestry of teamwork, the threads of adaptability and resilience are critical for creating a durable and dynamic picture. As much as we plan, prepare, and strategize, change is a constant companion on our journey towards collective success. Within this understanding lies the power to transform the inevitable flux into a force that propels teams forward.

To thrive in an ever-evolving landscape, teams must not only accept change but embrace it wholeheartedly. This requires a shift from viewing change as a disruptive force to recognizing it as a catalyst for growth and innovation. When change is welcomed, teams unlock the potential to re-evaluate processes, challenge assumptions, and iterate towards excellence.

Change often arrives unannounced, demanding an immediate response. However, the most successful teams are those that maintain a steady course, anchored by a clear vision, yet empowered by the agility to maneuver through uncharted waters. It's about having the foresight to anticipate shifts and the flexibility to adapt strategies and goals accordingly.

Indeed, flexibility is the cornerstone of adaptability. It's the willingness to pivot, to re-examine roles within the team, and to diversify approaches in the face of new information or circumstances. Flexibility isn't about a lack of commitment to objectives; rather, it's a commitment to achieving them in the most effective way possible, under the prevailing conditions.

Resilience, on the other hand, is born from the team's collective endurance and tenacity. It speaks to the capacity to encounter setbacks, disruptions, and failures, yet refuse to be defined by them. Resilient teams are not deterred by adversity; they see it as a bridge to cross on the way to their ultimate destination.

Integrating adaptability and resilience into the core of a team's ethos begins with leadership. Leaders who cultivate an environment where change is not feared but welcomed empower their team to take calculated risks and to innovate. They lead by example, showing that the response to change defines the character and competence of the team.

Equally important in embracing change is maintaining open lines of communication. When change looms, clear and honest dialogue ensures that team members are not left to navigate its implications alone. Instead, they are supported by a collective intelligence, a gathering of diverse insights that enriches the team's understanding and response to new situations.

Learning to be comfortable with uncertainty is another necessary skill in embracing change. Uncertainty can bring discomfort, but it also brings opportunities for learning and improvement. Teams that maintain a learning mindset see each change as a lesson, an opportunity to refine their skills, knowledge, and processes.

Building a safety net within the team furthers this sense of security amidst change. A safety net is the assurance that all team members have the backing of the collective, a fallback when taking the necessary leap into the unknown. This safety net fosters a culture of trust, where members feel secure to explore, adapt, and occasionally fail, without fear of repercussion.

Being proactive rather than reactive to change is also key. Teams that anticipate potential changes and prepare contingency plans are better positioned to navigate shifts smoothly. They convert potential chaos into a structured adaptation process, which results in minimal disruption and optimal performance.

To this end, scenario planning is an invaluable tool. It allows teams to explore varied outcomes and their implications, empowering them to make informed decisions rapidly when circumstances change. This forethought ensures that teams are not caught off guard, but rather, are equipped to transition seamlessly to alternate paths to success.

Moreover, embracing change as a constant means recognizing that each member may cope with change differently. Some may find change invigorating and adapt swiftly, while others may struggle. Team adaptability is strengthened when there is support for individual members' adaptive processes, acknowledging unique responses and facilitating their integration into the flow of change.

Celebration of small victories is also crucial in maintaining team morale amidst change. Publicly acknowledging when individuals or the team successfully navigate a change reinforces the behavior and mindset necessary for adaptability. It sends a powerful message that effort and adaptability are valued and recognized.

The journey through change is not always smooth, and at times the foundation of the team may shake. However, it's precisely these moments that can serve as the forge for stronger connections and a deeper sense of purpose. Teams that have weathered storms together form unbreakable bonds and cultivate a shared resilience that becomes the bedrock of their sustained success.

Ultimately, embracing change as a constant is about holding onto the vision that binds the team together while fluidly navigating the path to reach it. It's about trusting in the collective strength and embracing each twist and turn not as a detour but as a necessary part of the journey toward triumph. With each adaptation and each recovered step, the team becomes more accomplished, versatile, and ready for what lies ahead.

Building a Resilient Team Culture

Success in today's dynamic world demands not just strength but also adaptability and resilience among teams. A culture that fosters resilience is akin to cultivating a garden that is robust yet flexible enough to withstand unpredictable weather. To nurture such a culture, one must first understand that resilience isn't a single attribute but a tapestry woven from many threads of behavior, mindset, and process.

At the heart of a resilient team culture lies the shared understanding that setbacks are inevitable, and yet, they are stepping stones to growth. The collective embrace of this perspective is what sets a tenacious team apart from the rest. It is the recognition that when a team faces challenges, they have an opportunity to emerge stronger from the experiences, learning valuable lessons that fortify their resolve for future endeavors.

Building a resilient team begins with hiring practices and continues through every aspect of team interaction. Investing time and resources in individuals who are adaptable, who address challenges with a positive attitude, and who are committed to continuous improvement is invaluable. These individuals become the bedrock for a culture that can endure, evolve, and excel amid the tides of change.

Moreover, communication must remain the pulsating bloodline of a team. Open, transparent conversations where team members feel safe to express their thoughts, feelings, and ideas are essential for resilience. It is through communication that a team coordinates its response to adversity, sharing insights and strategies that might otherwise be overlooked in more rigid environments.

Leaders play an instrumental role. They must exemplify resilience by demonstrating balance — knowing when to be steadfast and when to be yielding. Their guidance can steer a team through arduous times, while their genuine confidence in the team's abilities can motivate members to push beyond their perceived limitations. Leadership is about empowering individuals to feel they are instrumental in the success and recovery of the team.

Trust serves as the foundation on which resilient teams are built. When team members trust each other, they share a bond that allows for accountability without blame, vulnerability without fear, and cooperation without reservation. This trust is not gifted; it is earned through consistency in actions, reliability in performance, and integrity in intent.

Mutual support and empathy are powerful allies of resilience. Understanding that everyone has unique strengths and weaknesses allows teams to support one another when challenges arise. Celebrating each member's contributions reinforces the notion that every individual is an integral part of the team's fabric, essential in withstanding trials and tribulations.

Resilience also requires a culture of innovation and flexibility. Teams that are encouraged to think creatively and to pilot new approaches develop agility. They are not shackled by the 'this is how it's always been done' mentality. Instead, they harness the variety of their experiences and perspectives to devise novel solutions. Embracing innovation means embracing the possibility of failure as a natural byproduct of experimenting, and thus a component of learning.

Furthermore, fostering resilience involves regular reflection and retrospection. By taking the time to look back upon challenges faced and obstacles overcome, a team can gain insights that streamline future responses to similar situations. This process of continual learning strengthens the team's resilience muscle.

The concept of resilience is closely tied to the ability to manage stress and to recover quickly from difficulties. This involves not only physical and mental well-being but also the emotional climate of the team. A team that prioritizes its members' health and acknowledges the importance of work-life balance builds a sustainable and energetic workforce that can face challenges head-on.

Recognition and celebration are also key to a resilient team culture. Acknowledging the small victories alongside the major achievements keeps morale high, even during tough times. In recognizing efforts, teams validate the hard work put forth and the resiliency displayed, which boosts the collective desire to persevere through future adversities.

Resilient teams are also characterized by their sense of shared vision and purpose. When a team understands the bigger picture and feels aligned with the organization's direction, they can adapt more easily to changes necessary to achieve long-term goals. This shared vision builds a resilient mindset that is focused on long-term success rather than being derailed by short-term setbacks.

In times of upheaval, resilient teams can pivot effectively, thanks to the foundations of flexibility they have built into their culture. Adaptability becomes part of the team's identity, prompting members to seek out opportunities for growth in the face of change, rather than to resist it with trepidation.

Finally, the cultivation of a resilient team culture is an ongoing process, not a one-time initiative. It requires commitment, attention, and nurturing. Regularly reviewing and updating processes, offering training and development to sustain high performance, and staying attuned to the evolving needs of team members are all part of maintaining and strengthening the culture of resilience.

In conclusion, building a resilient team culture means shaping an environment where adaptability, trust, innovation, support, learning, and celebration are not just encouraged but embedded in the very essence of the team. It is about creating a space where together, through storm and calm, the team stands unwavering, with a collective will that seeks triumph not just for the individual, but for the entirety of the group. It is here, in this fertile ground, that the power of togetherness blossoms into an unassailable force, fostering win-win scenarios for all.

Developing Flexibility and Learning from Setbacks

In the journey toward collective triumph, the ability to adapt quickly and learn from challenges is paramount. Flexibility is not just a desirable trait; it is an essential component of a thriving team dynamic. A key aspect of developing this agility lies in embracing the inevitability of setbacks as opportunities for growth. Individuals and teams alike must recognize that detours and hurdles are not barriers to success but are, in fact, integral to the learning process.

Every setback experienced by a team is a repository of lessons; what distinguishes a resilient team is its capacity to mine this rich vein of experiential knowledge. It involves dissecting what went wrong, identifying the factors within control, and making the necessary adjustments. When a team approaches setbacks with curiosity rather than defensiveness, they tap into innovative problem-solving that strengthens the fabric of the group.

It's important to note that developing flexibility isn't about being reactionary – it's about cultivating an anticipatory posture that allows for swift and informed action when unexpected changes occur. This forward-thinking approach requires constant vigilance and a willingness to pivot, underscoring the importance of maintaining a shared vision even as the path to achieving it may shift.

Within this fluid landscape, learning becomes a continuous endeavor. A hallmark of effective teams is their commitment to ongoing education, through formal training or informal knowledge sharing. The goal is not just to accumulate information but to integrate learning into the very way the team operates, ensuring that each member is equipped to adapt as needed.

One potent method of reinforcing learning is through reflection. Conducting regular retrospectives after projects or upon encountering obstacles grants teams the chance to pause and evaluate their performance. It is through this introspection that insights surface and get distilled into actionable plans that inform future efforts.

The narrative of persistence also features prominently when fostering flexibility. Teams that view their journey as a continuum rather than a series of disjointed events can build a stronger, more cohesive unit. They understand that every effort builds upon the last and that resilience is forged in the crucible of persistent endeavor.

Likewise, celebrating small victories in the face of setbacks is a powerful way to maintain morale and encourage flexibility. When a team stops to acknowledge the overcoming of obstacles, it reinforces the belief that no challenge is insurmountable and that each team member's contribution is valuable.

Moreover, an environment that supports taking calculated risks underpins the teaching that setbacks are indeed learning avenues. Risk-taking must be managed wisely, of course, but without it, opportunities for innovation and growth may be missed. It takes a secure team to step into the unknown, one where trust has been established and the cultural narrative is one of encouragement and support.

In the grand scheme, learning from setbacks is tantamount to honing one's instincts for decision-making. A team adept at navigating challenges is better positioned to make strategic choices in real-time, choices that align with the shared goals and vision of the team.

Ultimately, teams that embody flexibility and a learning-oriented mindset are those that not only survive but thrive. They move beyond mere resilience, becoming adaptable forces that can face any challenge, turn setbacks into stepping stones, and forge ahead toward collective success. The power of togetherness is most evident when a group learns, adapts, and grows together, crafting a narrative of achievement that is as dynamic as it is enduring.

Chapter 9:
Creating Win-Win Situations

In the journey to cultivate harmony within teams, the art of creating win-win situations is perhaps the most noble of pursuits. This chapter delves into the ethos of reciprocal success, asserting that the true measure of victory is not in one's isolated accomplishments, but in the collective flourishing of all stakeholders involved. Mastering negotiation skills that consider the aspirations and needs of each team member will lead to an unshakable foundation of partnership. It's about the alchemy of transforming individual potential into a consolidated powerhouse, with the understanding that synergy is not merely cooperative effort—rather, it's the embodiment of each person's strengths combined to achieve goals that seemed insurmountable alone. The spirit of this chapter lies in the belief that crafting solutions for mutual benefit is an inexhaustible source of innovation and progress, for when one wins in the context of the group's vision, we all triumph.

Negotiation Skills for Team Environments

In the spirit of fostering effective team environments, it's imperative to recognize the pivotal role that negotiation skills play in creating win-win situations. The art of negotiation within a team setting is less about competitive advantage and more about finding a common ground that benefits all parties involved. Crafting a collaborative atmosphere where ideas flourish and compromises are reached is essential to the thriving heartbeat of a team's success.

At the core of negotiation within teams is the fundamental understanding that when one member wins, the team as a whole steps closer to victory. It's here that we find the subtle dance between asserting individual needs and valuing the collective goal. It can be a delicate balance, but with the right approach, team members can learn to articulate their perspectives and listen deeply to others, forming the bedrock of mutual respect.

Effective negotiation within a team starts with preparation. Every team member must come to the table with not only a clear understanding of their own objectives but also a willingness to understand the needs and drivers of their teammates. Preparing for a negotiation requires an openness to possibilities and an eagerness to explore options beyond one's own initial stance.

A crucial aspect of team negotiation is communication. Clear, concise, and respectful dialogue is invaluable as it lays the groundwork for trust. When team members communicate effectively, they eliminate misunderstandings that could escalate into conflicts and instead pave the way for constructive resolutions that propel the team forward.

Another element that is often overlooked but pivotal in team negotiations is empathy. The ability to put oneself in another's shoes fosters an environment where solutions are not just about the bottom line but about connecting with one's colleagues on a human level. Empathy leads to deeper understanding and ultimately to agreements that consider everyone's well-being.

Active listening is, without question, a skill of immeasurable worth in negotiations. When team members truly listen to each other, they uncover needs and concerns that may not have been evident at first glance. Active listening also demonstrates respect and can help to diffuse tension, making it easier to find areas of agreement.

Strategic questioning during team negotiations helps in illuminating underlying interests and opening up dialogue for innovative solutions. Questions that delve deeper than surface issues invite contributions from all team members and lead to more comprehensive and inclusive results, ensuring that each voice is heard and valued.

To ensure that negotiations don't veer off into personal territories, setting ground rules can be a highly effective strategy. Ground rules might include maintaining professionalism, sticking to the topic at hand, and ensuring equal opportunity for contribution. These guidelines help to maintain focus and civility during discussions.

Negotiating in a team environment often means navigating diverse perspectives. Leveraging this diversity can lead to creative and high-quality outcomes. By combining diverse viewpoints and areas of expertise, teams can synthesize solutions that are more robust and innovative than any one member could conceive alone.

One of the most powerful tools in team negotiations is the principle of brainstorming. By fostering a non-judgmental space where every idea is welcome, teams can generate a plethora of options before narrowing down to the best solution. This approach avoids early criticism, which can often stifle creativity and seed unnecessary conflict.

An often overlooked yet critical negotiation skill for team environments is the art of concession-making. Understanding when and what to concede can turn a deadlock into a breakthrough. It demonstrates flexibility and goodwill, and when done strategically, it can enhance the team's long-term collaboration.

When it comes to decision-making, the power of consensus cannot be overstated. Reaching a unanimous agreement is not always feasible, but striving for consensus ensures that all team members have their say, and the final decision is one with which they can all live. This process minimizes resentment and fosters collective ownership of the outcome.

Even after a successful negotiation, the work of a team isn't finished. Follow-through is just as critical as the negotiation process itself. By keeping track of the agreements made and holding each other accountable, teams can ensure that decisions are implemented effectively, and the trust built during negotiations is fortified.

Finally, reflection after negotiations offers valuable insights for improvement. Teams that take the time to review their negotiation process can learn from their experiences, celebrating successes and identifying areas for development. This not only enhances future negotiations but also strengthens the team's capacity to work together cohesively.

Mastering negotiation skills in a team environment is not something that happens overnight. It requires patience, practice, and commitment from every team member. However, the rewards are substantial. When a team can navigate the complexities of negotiation with skill and grace, they unlock the door to endless possibilities, where their collective strength is more significant than the sum of its parts, and every victory is a shared triumph.

Building Synergy: Achieving More Together

In the pursuit of success, it's often said that two heads are better than one. This adage speaks to the very heart of synergy – where the collective power of a group surpasses the sum of individual efforts. Building synergy is not just about getting people to work together; it's about fostering an environment where collaboration naturally leads to greater outcomes for everyone involved.

Synergy arises from a web of relationships sustained by trust, commitment, and a shared vision. It's forged in the heat of shared challenges and strengthened through the mutual triumphs that come from overcoming them. When teams achieve synergy, they enter a realm of enhanced creativity, efficiency, and innovation that is unattainable in solitary endeavors.

The foundation of building such synergy is the establishment of common goals. These act as a compass that guides the collective efforts of the team, ensuring that each step taken is in harmony with the direction of the whole. This unity of purpose is the seed from which the fruit of collaborative success grows.

Individuals bring to the table a diverse array of skills, experiences, and perspectives. Building synergy means leveraging these unique attributes so that each member's strengths complement the others. When this intricate puzzle is assembled correctly, the picture that emerges is one of unparalleled collective capability.

Open lines of communication are essential for cultivating synergy. When team members communicate effectively, they understand not only the tasks at hand but also the motivations and ideas of their colleagues. Such understanding is the bedrock upon which strong relationships are built – a necessity for collaborative endeavor.

A synergistic team navigates conflict by turning potential stumbling blocks into stepping stones. It recognizes that disagreement, when approached constructively, can be a source of growth and innovation. These teams know the value of healthy debate and use it to refine their strategies and strengthen their bond.

True synergy cannot be mandated; it must be grown organically. It comes to life in an inclusive environment where every member feels valued and able to contribute. This sense of belonging is a powerful motivator – it drives individuals to invest in the team's vision and push beyond their limitations.

Moving towards synergy requires a leadership that is not confined to positions or titles but is a responsibility distributed among all members. Leaders in a synergistic team facilitate, inspire, and listen. They set an example by acting as stewards of the team's vision, empowering others to take initiative and make decisions.

Building synergy is an ongoing journey, not a destination. Just like a well-oiled machine, it requires consistent maintenance – recognition of efforts, recalibration of strategies, and realignment of goals. This ensures that the momentum of collaboration doesn't wane but rather strengthens over time.

Synergistic teams celebrate diversity, recognizing that the interplay of different ideas and approaches is fertile ground for creativity. They understand that innovation rarely comes from homogeneity but rather from the dynamic mix of minds working in concert.

Trust is the glue that holds a synergistic team together. It allows for vulnerability among members, fostering an environment where risks can be taken and innovation can thrive. A team rooted in trust is one where each member can rely on the others, creating an unshakable foundation for collective effort.

Motivation in a synergistic team is both intrinsic and extrinsic. Members are driven by personal passion as well as the desire to contribute to the group's success. The shared joy in achieving team goals further fuels individual commitment and team spirit.

Adaptability and resilience are hallmarks of a team with strong synergy. They are prepared to face change head-on, viewing it not as a threat but as an opportunity to evolve. This adaptability allows the team to navigate the unpredictable waters of the professional world with agility and grace.

As synergy within a team grows, so does its capacity to negotiate and craft solutions for mutual benefit. This paves the way for generating win-win situations, where all parties involved emerge better off. Such outcomes are emblematic of the highest level of teamwork.

In the final analysis, synergy embodies the philosophy that we can achieve more together than we can alone. It's the embodiment of the belief that when individual potential is linked with collective aspiration, the possibilities become endless. Building synergy is not just an endeavor in cooperation; it's a commitment to excellence through unity.

Crafting Solutions for Mutual Benefit

As we delve into the realms of collaboration, we come to understand that the resonance of mutual benefit is not only a pillar but an art in itself. True synergy is born when the whole becomes greater than the sum of its parts. Crafting solutions that cater to the interests of all stakeholders involved requires a delicate dance of negotiation, understanding, and inventive thinking.

Imagine a scenario where individual needs align seamlessly with the collective agenda. Such an outcome is not the result of happenstance, but the product of intentional design. It starts with the willingness to listen—to genuinely absorb the perspectives and necessities of those around us. This active listening is the cornerstone in developing a fertile ground where innovative solutions flourish.

One must enter negotiations with the purity of intent. It isn't about outmaneuvering one another but about building bridges that connect differing viewpoints. The power lies in the transformative approach that instead of dividing the pie differently, seeks to make the pie bigger for everyone. This is where creativity becomes paramount; the inciting of new ideas or unconventional approaches that disrupt traditional zero-sum game mentality.

Employing empathy is crucial in this process. By understanding the motivations that drive the parties involved, one can architect solutions that are not only effective but also empathetic. It transcends the transactional nature of deal-making into a transformational experience that bonds teams and enhances relationships. It's about crafting a narrative where everyone sees their reflection in the outcome—a shared victory.

Transparent communication needs to stand at the helm as teams navigate through the process. It acts as a tether that keeps motives aligned and misunderstandings at bay. An environment where thoughts and suggestions are welcomed and valued serves as an incubator for mutual benefit. The core objective remains to attain a resolution that is embraced by all—not enforced upon a reluctant minority.

Alongside this, the cultivation of patience must not be underestimated. These finely-tuned resolutions don't appear out of thin air but emerge from the smelting of ideas over time. Patience is what allows these ideas to mature into a coherent solution that culminates in shared success.

It's important to recognize that crafting these win-win scenarios also requires a degree of pragmatism. Not all ideas will be viable and not all negotiations will result in perfect equilibrium. Yet, this is where teams can display their mettle by prioritizing what benefits the group and upholds the integrity of the team's vision.

The currency of mutual benefit is trust. As team members come to realize that the ecosystem they operate in is fortified with fairness and consideration, they are more likely to invest themselves wholly. This trust catalyzes collective effort and diminishes the silos of self-interest that can often derail team objectives.

Finally, it is the celebration of these shared victories that reinforce the value of mutual benefit. It becomes a self-perpetuating cycle—success breeds success. As one solution paves the way for the next, the team develops a rhythmic competence in not just meeting challenges but transforming them into opportunities for growth and innovation.

Thus, in this intricate web of dependencies that define our interactions, we find that the capability to craft solutions for mutual benefit is not just about achieving goals but about elevating the human experience within a team. It's understanding that together, we don't just aim for the stars—we sculpt constellations.

Chapter 10:
Conflict Resolution: Turning
Tensions into Triumphs

Amid the quest for harmony within teams, conflict is as inevitable as the rising sun, yet it harbors a potent seed of opportunity – the chance to forge stronger bonds, hone problem-solving skills, and uplift collective performance. Encountering friction with a mindset rooted in valor and a heart aiming for unity can transform discord into a catalyst for growth. Employing active listening, empathy, and negotiation, teams can traverse the treacherous terrain of disagreement and emerge on the other side with solutions that resonate with shared values. It's in these very moments of challenge that a team's character is tested and its resilience built. As we pull from the wellspring of diversity and channel the power of varying perspectives, conflicts cease to be deadlocks and become stepping stones to innovate, to discover, to triumph - together.

Identifying Sources of Conflict

As teams journey toward collective goals, it is inevitable that conflicts will arise. While often painted in a negative light, the seeds of conflict can sprout opportunities for growth and understanding, if approached with an astute eye for their sources. Uncovering the roots of discord prepares the groundwork for sustainable resolutions that foster togetherness and ensure that each team member's voice contributes to a harmonious symphony.

One primary source of conflict within teams is miscommunication. Simple misunderstandings or a lack of clear dialogue pave the way for mistrust and assumptions that can twist the narrative of intentions. It is crucial to cultivate a climate where open communication is not just encouraged but integral to the team's ethos. When expectations are communicated explicitly, and everyone is on the same wavelength, much of this potential conflict dissipates into the ether.

Differing values and beliefs may also sow the seeds of discord. In a tapestry woven with diverse threads, each color speaks to a unique background and perspective. While this diversity strengths the fabric's overall resilience, it can also lead to clashes when deeply held convictions meet. Respectful acknowledgment and appreciation of these differences are vital, nurturing an environment where varied beliefs foster innovation rather than ignite tension.

Personality clashes are yet another culprit of unrest. Not every individual's modus operandi harmonizes effortlessly with others. What fuels one may drain another, leading to friction. Awareness and acceptance of these personal styles can aid in orchestrating a balanced approach where each member's traits are leveraged, enabling the team to thrive amidst individual idiosyncrasies.

Resource constraints and competition can also be a breeding ground for conflict. When members vie for limited tools or recognition, the situation can turn adversarial. In such scenarios, reminding the team of shared goals and the big picture can act as a soothing balm, easing tensions volatilized by the scramble for scarce commodities.

Role ambiguity serves as another potential disruptor. Without clear definitions and expectations of each member's function within a team, overlapping duties or a lack of responsibility can ferment discontent. Careful crafting of roles and responsibilities with input from all team members ensures that everyone has a clear purpose and direction, minimizing the risk of conflicts born from uncertainty.

Unmet expectations can also stir the pot of dissent. When individual aims don't align with team results, frustration and disillusionment can seep in. Aligning personal ambitions with collective outcomes through regular check-ins and adaptive planning can create a resilient framework that withstands such pressures.

Process and structural conflicts can arise from inefficiencies or organizational inconsistencies. When the system within which the team operates is flawed, it can lead to unnecessary roadblocks. Ironing out these structural issues requires a proactive stance towards continuous improvement and a willingness to adapt to more effective processes.

The perception of unfairness or inequality can cut deeply into a team's trust fabric. Whether rooted in workload disparities, recognition, or opportunities, perceived injustice is a quick catalyst for unhappiness. Ensuring equitable practices and transparent decision-making processes is an antidote to such potentially toxic situations.

Lack of accountability can cause rifts within teams. When members do not take ownership of their actions or the actions of the collective, blame games commence, and solidarity crumbles. Cultivating a culture where everyone is held to their commitments and takes responsibility for both triumphs and trials strengthens the trust tying a team together.

External pressures, such as economic shifts, industry changes, or competitive dynamics, can indirectly incite conflict as everyone struggles to navigate the choppy waters of change. Staying united, with an emphasis on clear and frequent communication about external factors, can help mitigate the internal strife that these pressures might otherwise ignite.

Leadership styles can also play a part in either quelling or fanning the flames of conflict. A leader's approach to guidance, delegation, and feedback can significantly influence the team's harmony. Leaders who foster inclusivity and practice empathy often steer their teams through turbulent waters with more grace than those who rule with an iron fist.

Lastly, personal stress and burnout can spill over into professional domains, igniting conflicts as side effects of larger personal challenges. Acknowledging and addressing the needs for personal well-being and work-life balance can pre-empt these personal struggles from becoming team issues.

Conflict, while inherent to the human experience, need not be an insurmountable obstacle. It is an indication of the dynamic interplay of ideas, personalities, and goals within a team. By identifying the sources of conflict and understanding their roots, teams can devise strategies to harness these tensions, channeling them into creative solutions and opportunities for collective growth. Thus, conflict becomes a catalyst for triumph rather than a barrier to success.

As teams learn to identify and address the multifaceted sources of conflicts, they pave the way for a culture where open-mindedness, empathy, and proactive problem-solving reign supreme. This begins a journey not just toward the resolution of conflicts but toward a profound transformation in the very nature of how teams interact, collaborate, and succeed together.

Techniques for Constructive Confrontation

Within the tapestry of team dynamics, tensions are, perhaps, the threads that test the strength of the whole fabric. It isn't the presence of conflict that can unravel progress, but rather the manner in which it is confronted. Constructive confrontation is an art that, when mastered, transforms potential discord into a symphony of collaboration. The following techniques aim to reshuffle the deck of discord, turning confrontations into stepping stones for team triumph.

At the heart of constructive confrontation lies active listening. One must not only hear but understand the sentiments behind the words of the other party. Listening with empathy allows individuals to connect with each other's perspectives, fostering an environment where solutions can be cultivated from mutual understanding. It is the base from which bridges of agreement can be built.

Clear communication is the beacon that guides ships safely through the stormy seas of disagreement. It's essential to articulate thoughts and feelings without ambiguity, ensuring every message sent is the message received. Be succinct and direct, yet considerate – this approach fosters clarity and helps avoid unnecessary misunderstandings that can escalate conflicts.

Maintaining clear and respectful boundaries is like setting the rules of engagement before a duel. It ensures that all parties understand the limits of the confrontation, keeping discussions on-topic and preventing personal attacks, which can lead to lasting resentment and a breakdown in team cohesion.

Embracing a growth mindset in the face of conflict involves seeing every conflict as an opportunity to learn and improve, not just as a problem to be solved. This perspective opens avenues for innovative solutions that can strengthen the team and enhance its performance.

The use of "I" statements rather than "you" accusations is a subtle yet powerful shift in language that can transform a potentially combative situation into a collaborative exchange. This technique promotes ownership of one's feelings and dissuades defensiveness, allowing for more fruitful discussions.

Finding common ground is often the first step toward resolution. Teams that identify shared values or goals can use these as a compass to navigate through tumultuous confrontations towards constructive outcomes. This commonality becomes the glue that holds the team together, even when opinions diverge.

Encouraging a solution-focused mindset within confrontation steers the team away from dwelling on the problem and towards the co-creation of possible solutions. This proactive approach builds momentum and directs energy positively, fostering a sense of shared accomplishment.

It is important to acknowledge emotions but not be governed by them. Recognizing the emotional content within a confrontation allows for a humanized approach to problem-solving, but it's crucial to not let emotions override logic and reason – a balance must be struck for effective resolution.

Timing can be the unsung hero of confrontations. Approaching a heated issue when all parties are calm and prepared to engage meaningfully can significantly improve the chances of a positive outcome. Conversely, forcing a confrontation in the heat of the moment often leads to escalation rather than resolution.

Incorporating break periods during intense discussions can serve as an emotional reset button, providing the space and time required for individuals to process information and cool down. This can prevent the buildup of stress and maintain a level of civility during the dialogue.

Knowing when to seek external support or mediation can be a critical judgement call. Sometimes an impartial perspective can shed new light on a conflict and guide the path to resolution. It's a sign of strength, not weakness, to enlist help when the situation demands it.

Reflective summarization is a method where the key points and emotions expressed by each party are reiterated. This technique ensures that all participants feel heard and understood, and it can also help to unravel misunderstandings that might be driving the conflict.

Flexibility in the approach to confrontation is akin to the pliability of willow branches in the wind – less prone to breaking, more likely to survive the storm. Being open to alternate methods of communication and resolution is essential for adapting to the ever-changing landscape of team dynamics.

Finally, committing to a follow-up after the confrontation ensures that the agreed-upon solutions are implemented and any residual feelings are addressed. It reinforces the team's dedication to maintaining harmony and continuous improvement in their working relationships.

Conflict is an inevitable part of human interaction, especially within teams striving toward a shared goal. But when approached with the aforementioned techniques, confrontation becomes an instrument of growth rather than disruption. It provides a foundation upon which triumphs may be built, securing the strength of the team and propelling it towards collective success.

Transforming Challenges into Team-Strengthening Opportunities

In the quest for team success, understanding that challenges pave the way for growth and strength is pivotal. Within the fabric of cooperation lies the thread of adversity, which when pulled, can either unravel the team or tighten its bonds. To ensure the latter, it is vital to approach obstacles as catalysts for development, fostering a culture where each setback serves as a stepping stone towards collective resilience.

Team dynamics are frequently tested in the crucible of difficulty. Yet, it is here that the opportunity to redefine and rediscover collaborative potential is most potent. As conflicts arise, they bring forth the raw material needed to build an edifice of stronger relationships and improved processes. It is about turning the tide of adversity, making it the impetus for enhanced trust and communication. This transformative approach galvanizes team members, inspiring them to navigate challenges with a unified front.

Each challenge encountered by a team is a chance to put their foundational values - trust, mutual respect, and shared vision - to the test. Valuing each member's voice during trying times reinforces the principle that every perspective is a cornerstone in the team's collective wisdom. An effective leader will guide the dialogue, ensuring that all contributions are channeled towards a common goal, and appreciating the diversity of thoughts and solutions presented.

Maintaining an environment where challenges are openly discussed and learned from ensures that no member stands alone when facing them. Encourage the team to reflect on setbacks just as they would celebrate victories. It's about fostering an atmosphere where accountability is shared and vulnerabilities can be expressed without fear of reprisal. This transparency is empowering and underscores the essence of a coherent and supportive unit.

In moments when discord seems imminent, recall the instruments for healthy dispute resolution. Crafting amicable solutions requires negotiation skills, the capacity to empathize with differing viewpoints, and a steadfast commitment to reaching a mutually beneficial outcome. A well-resolved conflict fortifies the team's framework, teaching members to face future challenges with confidence and a sense of preparedness.

Moreover, the cultivation of diversity within the team is not merely about including various backgrounds and skill sets; it is about actively leveraging these differences to forge innovative solutions to problems. When confronted with an obstacle, the assortment of experiences transforms into a rich reservoir of ideas, from which the team can draw unique and effective strategies.

Resilience is a trait that gets sharper with each challenge faced; it is not inherent but cultivated through the continuous cycle of falling and rising together as a team. A resilient team can adapt and bounce back, taking not just survival but thriving to heart. Demonstrating adaptability and the willingness to learn from every situation instills the kind of spirit that distinguishes good teams from great ones.

Motivation and enthusiasm play a crucial role in maneuvering through team challenges. Recognize the efforts and mental strength required to surmount these hurdles. Celebrating the small victories achieved on the path to overcoming difficulties is just as important as rejoicing in reaching significant milestones. This recognition nurtures a sense of achievement and fuels the collective drive to confront and conquer future trials.

Ultimately, embracing challenges as opportunities requires a deliberate shift in mindset, from viewing them as obstacles to regarding them as integral elements of the quest for excellence. It is a journey where collaboration becomes not just a strategy but a value, a belief that together, obstacles are not so much impediments as they are gateways to team strengthening and unparalleled success.

Thus, as teams encounter and work through challenges, they script a narrative of transformation and unity. Turning tensions into triumphs, the team emerges not just intact but invigorated, with fortified bonds and an unshakeable conviction that together, they can turn any challenge into an opportunity to grow stronger, more cohesive, and more victorious.

Chapter 11:
From Good to Great: Boosting Team Performance

In the pursuit of excellence, teams often find themselves at a crossroads where good is no longer good enough. Elevating a team from good to great demands a strategic approach that encompasses continuous assessment and development of team dynamics. The true alchemy of high-performing teams lies in their ability to not just focus on outcomes but to commit to the journey of relentless improvement. By nurturing an environment of continuous learning and growth, leaders can foster a culture where feedback is not merely accepted but sought after as a catalyst for change. It's crucial to recognize that grand results stem from an accumulation of small, consistent steps. This chapter dives into the essence of amplifying team performance, sculpting a resilient and adaptive group that not only meets expectations but soars beyond them, turning every obstacle into a stepping stone towards unmatched excellence.

Assessing and Improving Team Dynamics

The journey from good to great is laden with the incessant need to assess and refine the dynamic flow of a team's lifeblood. It is through the thorough evaluation of how a team ticks that one can spark transformational shifts and optimize performance. This endeavor requires a meticulous understanding of interpersonal relations and how they align with collective objectives.

First, one must take a step back to observe the team as a whole. Consider the unique blend of personalities, the ebb and flow of communication, and the ever-present undercurrent of team morale. Are there signs of dissonance within the ranks, or is there a harmonic synchrony that propels the team forward? Understanding these aspects lays the ground for improvement.

Diving deeper, the efficacy of team dynamics can often hinge on the subtleties of trust and transparency. Does each team member feel comfortable sharing ideas and concerns? A foundation of trust bolsters a team's resilience and capacity to collaborate, confronting challenges with a unified front.

Mutual respect and diversity are also instrumental in augmenting team dynamics. Recognizing and leveraging the array of backgrounds, skills, and viewpoints within the team can stimulate innovation and lead to solutions that are robust and well-rounded. Inclusivity is not mere policy, but a strategic advantage.

Shared goals and vision are the magnetic forces that draw disparate individuals into a cohesive, strong team. These elements should be revisited regularly to ensure that the team's compass is well calibrated and pointing towards common aspirations. The alignment of personal ambitions with the team's objectives fosters a sense of purpose and direction.

When performance seems to plateau, it is often a signal to re-evaluate and realign. Embark on a collective introspection to identify if every member's strengths are utilized optimally. A team that meshes individual prowess with the collective good will find itself operating on a higher plane.

Communication is the heart through which the lifeblood of the team flows. It needs to be open, candid, and, most importantly, effective. Teams must cultivate an environment where dialogue crisscrosses freely, allowing individuals to voice their insights and reservations without fear of reproach.

Navigational skills in conflict and consensus building are essential for a thriving team. Disagreements, when approached with the right attitude and tools for healthy resolution, can give rise to stronger ties and a deeper understanding of each other's perspectives.

Leadership is the rudder that guides a team through the tumultuous seas of collaboration. But this is not the domain of a select few. Leadership must be distributed, enabling each team member to take the helm when their particular skills are called for, thus cultivating a culture of shared responsibility and initiative.

Diversity is a wellspring of creativity and must be embraced wholly. Creating rich tapestries from the assorted strands of cultural, intellectual, and experiential backgrounds available can set the stage for wonderful symphonies of innovation.

Trust and vulnerability go hand in hand within teams. It is in being open about one's limitations and accountable for one's actions that a supportive and robust framework for teamwork is built. This framework becomes the safe space where risks are taken and growth occurs.

Motivation and a strong team spirit can be the wind in the sails propelling a team towards greatness. Understanding what drives each member and fostering a collective spirit of dedication and enthusiasm can help a team weather the doldrums of complacency.

When adversity strikes, it is the adaptability and resilience of a team that dictates its survival and success. Building these qualities involves learning from setbacks, developing flexibility, and embracing change as an inevitable component of the journey.

Negotiation skills and the art of achieving synergy are critical in elevating a team from merely functioning to thriving. Crafting solutions that bring mutual benefit ensures that the team operates not as solitary agents but as a unit that achieves more together.

Once the assessment is complete and the areas for improvement identified, the work begins in earnest. Systematic implementation of changes, continuous reassessment, and a steadfast commitment to grow together can morph good teams into great ones. Allowing them to transcend previous limitations and soar to new heights, these efforts encapsulate the power of synergy and the essence of togetherness—a synergy that creates win-win scenarios for every member and the team as a whole.

Continuous Learning and Growth

In the pursuit of transforming from good to great, it becomes imperative to embrace continuous learning and growth within a team. The journey towards greatness requires a commitment to perpetual self-improvement and a culture that prioritizes the evolution of its members. In this quest, a team must recognize the value of knowledge as the foundation upon which its future successes are built.

A cornerstone of this learning ethos is the team's ability to look inward and harness the collective drive for advancement. Empowering each member to take ownership of their growth trajectory not only serves as a catalyst for personal development but also fortifies the team's overall capability. The synergistic effect of these developments ushers in an era of innovation and agility.

The importance of creating an environment conducive to learning cannot be overstated. An ambience that encourages curiosity and allows individuals to openly share experiences, ideas, and knowledge, catapults the growth of both individuals and the collective. Such an environment is rich with dialogue, where each conversation becomes a stepping stone towards greater understanding and mastery.

Setting audacious goals for the group and for each member is equally essential. Goals that not only challenge the status quo but also excite the imagination instigate progress. These aspirations provide a north star, guiding each stride towards skill enhancement and the pursuit of excellence. They allow a team to transcend complacency and strive for new heights.

Proactively identifying skill gaps within the team is a strategic approach to continuous improvement. Addressing these areas promptly ensures that the group remains relevant and prepared to meet evolving demands. Tailoring learning experiences to individual needs emphasizes the value placed on each team member's contribution to the group's success.

Fostering a mindset of adaptability is a fundamental aspect of continuous learning. Challenges and changes in the work environment are inevitable; they are the forge upon which the steel of a great team is tempered. Embracing these uncertainties with a learning mentality transforms potential hurdles into opportunities for refinement and innovation.

Investing in regular training programs and educational resources signifies a committed effort towards collective competency and expertise. Be it workshops, seminars, or online courses, these tools become the instruments by which a team can fine-tune their skills and acquire new knowledge. This investment of time and resources into education reflects a deliberate strategy for long-term excellence.

Learning also extends beyond formal education to include reflection on past experiences. This reflective practice allows a team to analyze successes and, more importantly, understand failures. It provides invaluable insights into performance, driving improvements in strategies and process efficiencies. The collective intelligence of the team thus becomes greater than the sum of its parts.

Mentorship and coaching are yet another facet of the learning ecosystem within a team. Experienced members offering guidance to less experienced colleagues establish a tradition of knowledge sharing and personal investment in each other's success. This act of passing the torch fosters a sense of unity and trust, as well as the direct transfer of tacit knowledge.

Recognition of learning achievements acts as a powerful motivator. Celebrating milestones in personal and team development reinforces the value of continuous learning. It serves as a public acknowledgement of the effort put into growth and also sets a precedent for others to follow.

Implementing mechanisms for continuous feedback is crucial to the learning process. Feedback systems that are constructive and timely pave the way for adjustments to be made before challenges escalate. They provide the necessary navigational aids for the team to steer their learning journey on course and make real-time improvements.

Building a repository of learning materials and instituting a knowledge management system allow for the preservation and dissemination of collective wisdom. This reservoir becomes a touchstone for current and future team members, enabling them to draw upon accumulated experiences and expertise seamlessly.

Lastly, the spirit of continuous learning and growth must extend beyond the workplace. Encouraging team members to pursue personal interests and passions that stimulate intellectual and emotional growth ensures that they bring a well-rounded perspective to the team. This diversity of thought and experience is invaluable in forging a team that is not only proficient but also insightful and visionary in its approach.

In conclusion, lifting a team from good to great lies in the untiring pursuit of growth and learning. It is an unending journey marked by the team's commitment to each other's and their own development. As each member becomes more knowledgeable and skilled, the team itself becomes more capable, adaptable, and resilient, setting the stage for unparalleled success and achievement.

The next steps beckon with the promise of continuous growth, as each lesson learned and skill acquired magnifies the potency of the collective. A relentless pursuit of progress, focused on nurturing a culture of learning, ensures that the journey from good to great is not just possible but inevitable. In doing so, a team shapes not only its destiny but also leaves a legacy of excellence for those who follow.

Implementing Effective Feedback Systems is an essential part of the continuous learning and growth chapter in the journey towards superlative team performance. A well-designed feedback system serves as the mirror for a team, providing reflections that, although sometimes uncomfortable, are necessary for personal and collective development. It sets the stage for open dialogue, where members can offer and receive constructive consultations that help refine skills, behaviors, and processes.

In the pursuit of crafting such an invaluable tool, one must first understand the nature and purpose of feedback within the team context. Feedback is more than just a mechanism for improvement; it is an affirmation of commitment to one another's growth. To be effective, feedback must be timely, specific, and balanced. It should offer clear insights into what is working well and what requires adjustment without disregarding the emotional impact it might have on its recipients.

One of the cornerstones of a successful feedback system is creating a culture where feedback is not just accepted but sought. Every member should feel empowered to ask for feedback as much as they are encouraged to provide it. This mutual exchange elevates the team's performance, for it transforms feedback from a top-down directive to a shared responsibility.

Critical to this process is the establishment of regular feedback loops. These can take various forms, from structured meetings and reviews, to informal discussions and peer-to-peer check-ins. Ensuring that feedback becomes a routine part of your team's operation removes the stigma and tension often associated with it, and instead embeds it into the natural rhythm of team life.

When implementing these systems, specificity cannot be overemphasized. Vague comments or generalized commendations do little to guide or motivate. Instead, team members should be equipped to provide actionable insights that directly relate to the task or behavior in question. This kind of precision requires attention to detail and a willingness to engage deeply with one another's work.

Balance, however, is equally important. Positive reinforcement has a key role in motivating team members and nurturing a positive team environment. Recognizing what someone has done well not only boosts confidence but also sets a standard for excellence within the team. Conversely, when offering suggestions for improvement, it should be done constructively, with an emphasis on solutions and support.

Feedback should also be a two-way street, including upwards feedback that challenges traditional hierarchies. When team members can give feedback to their leaders, it fosters an atmosphere of mutual respect and continuous improvement at all levels. Leaders themselves must model the vulnerability that they wish to see in their teams by accepting and acting on the feedback they receive.

Lastly, an effective feedback system must be underscored by follow-through. Feedback without subsequent action is like a map that leads nowhere. It is imperative that both givers and receivers of feedback commit to specific actions and support each other in their implementation. By visibly incorporating feedback into work practices, a team shows its dedication to actualizing its potential.

Realizing the implementation of an effective feedback system may require time and patience, but the rewards far outweigh the initial investment of effort. As a living process, a feedback mechanism can evolve with your team, continually adapting and refining itself to better serve its members and their shared goals. With attention and care, feedback becomes less of a task and more of a privilege—a sign of trust and a catalyst for transformation that underpins not only the achievements of the team but also the individual triumphs of its members.

At the heart of it all, effective feedback is a testimony to the power of togetherness. When every member of the group is committed to both giving and receiving honest, constructive feedback, the team enters a virtuous cycle of growth, resilience, and achievement. This dynamic sets the groundwork for any collective to reach beyond good and strive for greatness—a true manifestation of creating win-win scenarios for everyone involved.

Chapter 12:
Celebrating Success and Embracing New Horizons

As we turn the page to Chapter 12, "Celebrating Success and Embracing New Horizons," we reflect on the jubilant culmination of our collaborative efforts and look eagerly ahead to the promise of future endeavors. The journey of a team is marked by milestones that serve not only as proof of progress but also as beacons that inspire continued pursuit of excellence. In this chapter, we delve into the art of recognizing these pivotal moments with the grace and enthusiasm they deserve, ensuring that every member feels valued and empowered. Furthermore, we set our sights beyond the current triumphs to the vast expanse of opportunities that lie on the horizon. Embracing the new challenges that await, we prepare to carry forward the momentum we have built, as a team committed to elevating our collective aspirations to new heights. Let's revel in our hard-earned victories while harnessing the invigorating energy of anticipated successes, poised to achieve an even greater impact together.

Recognizing Milestones and Sharing Success Stories

Achieving milestones within a team is akin to scaling a peak - it's a moment to pause, reflect, and recognize the path traveled. To truly celebrate success and embrace new horizons, it is essential that every step taken be acknowledged and shared. The sharing of success stories is not merely about basking in the glow of achievement, but about setting the stage for future endeavors and inspiring continuous growth.

Acknowledging individual and team milestones reinforces the significance of personal and shared goals. Whether small steps or giant leaps, these accomplishments serve as tangible progress markers that bolster morale. It's an opportunity for teams to come together in a collective expression of gratitude, pride, and recognition of the efforts poured into reaching those goals.

Sharing success stories is incredibly powerful. These narratives serve as motivational beacons, often igniting the drive in others to pursue their own aspirations. These stories transcend mere anecdotes; they become part of the team's vibrant legacy. Such stories are compelling not only due to the triumphs they recount, but because they lay bare the struggles overcome along the way.

There's no denying the emotional resonance of success stories. They create connections on a profound level, engendering an environment where individuals see their achievements as vital contributions to the team's overall success. In sharing these stories, a narrative tapestry is woven, one that binds the team and fortifies its collective identity.

But beyond mere story-telling, celebrating milestones often entails ceremonies or rituals that give a sense of closure to one chapter and an enthusiastic opening to the next. Employee recognition programs, celebratory gatherings, and public commendations are all ways teams can shine a light on the accomplishments that propel them forward.

In recognizing achievements, it is important to maintain balance. Focus must be equally allocated between celebrating high performers and recognizing team players who may not be in the limelight but whose contributions are equally vital. Such equitable acknowledgment ensures that every team member feels valued and seen.

As milestones are celebrated and success stories shared, there lies a potent opportunity to reflect on the journey. It's a time to analyze what worked and what didn't, thereby gleaning insights that can shape strategies moving forward. Learning from these experiences collaboratively arms the team with wisdom for future challenges.

Recognition further solidifies the principles of trust and transparency within the team. Open acknowledgment of each other's efforts strengthens bonds and builds a robust team dynamic, one where every contribution is not only recognized but also expected and encouraged.

When success is shared, it promotes a culture of collective achievement. As team members see their peers recognized, a healthy sense of competition is fostered, motivating them to strive for their own success stories - which, when realized, will further contribute to the team's legacy of accomplishments.

While it's essential to celebrate, it is equally important to use these occasions to reset and prepare for the next set of goals. Success is not a final destination but rather a signpost along an ever-evolving journey of growth and improvement. By acknowledging both the peaks and the plateaus, teams can better navigate the landscape of their ambitions.

Sharing success naturally begets more successes, as a culture of recognition makes way for a culture of performance. In an environment where achievements are celebrated, team members are more likely to invest their best efforts, secure in the knowledge that their contributions are valued and their milestones, no matter the size, will be recognized.

Ultimately, recognizing milestones and sharing success stories serve to build an overall resilient team. It fosters an atmosphere where although individual members may falter, the team as a unit perseveres, buoyed by the strength of its collective achievements and the shared vision of what success looks like.

Moreover, success stories are not mere recounts of achievements but are also articulations of a team's identity. These stories define who the team is and what it stands for. They are constant reminders that every individual is part of something much larger than themselves - a team that triumphs together.

Every chapter of success written into the annals of a team's history paves the way for the next. Recognizing milestones is thus not just about looking back with satisfaction, but about looking forward with determination and the unwavering belief that there is much more to achieve, and together, it is all within reach.

In uniting to share success stories, teams don't just acknowledge the road traveled; they map out the path ahead. They build a narrative of persistence, collaboration, and mutual support that stands the test of time and emboldens every member to reach further, grow stronger, and together, scale new and extraordinary horizons.

The Next Steps: Sustaining Momentum

After achieving a commendable milestone, it's easy to bask in the glory of success. However, the true test of a successful team lies in its ability to sustain that momentum. Forward motion is the lifeblood of progress, and without it, even the most spirited of teams can stall. As we embrace new horizons, it's imperative that we keep our collective eyes fixed on the future and move deliberately towards it.

Sustaining momentum requires that each member of the team understands the vision of where the team is headed. Clarity in direction ensures that everyone is rowing in the same unison towards the desired destination. Like a lighthouse guiding ships through the darkness, a clear vision serves as a beacon, keeping the team's journey on course.

Growth is an integral part of maintaining momentum. Teams that remain stagnant inevitably fall behind. Therefore, fostering a culture of continuous improvement is critical. This means actively seeking out opportunities for learning and development. By doing so, the team doesn't just rest on their laurels but builds upon them.

In the celebration of success, the fire of ambition should not be allowed to wane. It is the drive to achieve more, to conquer new challenges, that propels teams forward. This fire must be kindled and nurtured, ensuring it burns vividly in the hearts of all team members. Ambition fuels action, and it's through actionable steps that momentum is maintained.

However, ambition without a plan is merely a wish. That's why goal setting is paramount. Short-term, achievable goals can serve as stepping stones towards more audacious targets. Checks and balances should be instituted not as means of control, but as guiding rails to ensure that the team's efforts are aligned and purposeful.

Accountability is another cornerstone of sustaining momentum. When every team member is accountable for their actions and understands their role in the larger picture, a powerful sense of ownership is cultivated. This ownership is the difference between 'someone should do' and 'I will do.' Encouraging individuals to take charge fosters an environment where progress is everyone's responsibility.

Recognition is a powerful motivator. Celebrating small victories along the way provides the team with the morale boost needed to push forward. It serves as a reminder that their efforts are valued and crucial to the overall goal. Strong teams do not underestimate the power of pausing to applaud each other's endeavours. Such moments are not just breaks in the race; they are the very fuel that enables the long-distance run.

Communication remains vital in the quest to keep the wheel turning. A team that communicates effectively is well-positioned to identify bottlenecks and brainstorm on ways to overcome them. Open channels of dialogue ensure that ideas flow freely, problems are addressed promptly, and the team's unity remains unshaken.

In the wake of success, complacency becomes a subtle yet formidable adversary. Teams must guard against the seductive comfort of the status quo. The relentless pursuit of excellence is what differentiates good teams from great ones. It is a pursuit that requires persistence, a trait that is indispensable in the journey to sustained achievements.

Change is an ever-constant factor in any dynamic team environment. Embracing change and harnessing its power is a testament to a team's ability to thrive. Adaptable teams can pivot when necessary, transforming potential hurdles into opportunities for growth and learning. The ability to evolve with changing circumstances keeps the team relevant and dynamic.

Leadership continues to play a pivotal role in propelling the team forward. Leaders must be beacons of inspiration, embodying the team's mission and values. They need to effectively steer efforts, fostering a spirit of innovation and pushing the team to explore new territories. Good leaders inspire, but great leaders empower, turning every team member into a champion for progress.

Celebrating success shouldn't signal the end, but rather serve as a launching pad for the next chapter. Reflection is a powerful tool that allows a team to not only appreciate how far they've come but also to critically analyze paths that lead to future accomplishments. Evaluation of past achievements is a stepping stone for setting even higher standards.

Energy management is as crucial as any other resource within the team. High productivity and perpetual activities could eventually lead to burnout. Teams that sustain momentum know when to accelerate and when to pace themselves. Just as a well-tuned engine is mindful of the balance between power and efficiency, so must the team be in its exertions.

In closing, sustaining momentum isn't the responsibility of a select few but a collective effort. It necessitates a shared mindset, a synergy of purpose, and a commitment to traverse the path that lies ahead. The journey may be rife with unknowns, but with a team unified in aspiration and action, the momentum generated will propel the team to new pinnacles of success.

As we look to the future, let's carry forward the lessons learned, the strengths acquired, and the inspirations gained. Together, we are poised not only to reach new heights but to redefine them. The next steps we take are not just strides towards personal or team goals, they are steps towards a legacy of excellence that inspires all to believe in the power of togetherness and the strength of collective endeavor.

Planning for Future Achievements as a Team involves setting a foundation that is as firm in foresight as it is in action. It is not merely about celebrating past triumphs but also about charting a course for continuous collective success. This endeavor requires a synchronized approach where the aspirations of individuals align with the objectives of the group, creating a roadmap for advancement that everyone can follow and contribute to.

Looking ahead demands that we understand the importance of setting attainable yet ambitious goals together. As a team, leveraging each member's unique strengths and insights to identify future opportunities plays a pivotal role in crafting a vision that is not only aspirational but also actionable. It's about asking not just where we want to be, but recognizing the steps it will take to get there.

Setting these goals as a group nurtures a sense of ownership and accountability. Each member becomes a stakeholder in the team's future, and this collective investment is a powerful motivator. When individuals are involved in planning, their personal commitment to team objectives increases, and as a result, their efforts align more closely with achieving shared milestones.

Strategic planning sessions are invaluable in this process. These gatherings offer a platform where creative ideas can flourish, and varied perspectives are acknowledged. Encouraging every team member to voice their vision and concerns fosters an environment where the seeds of innovation can germinate. Here, a team's diversity becomes its strength, as different experiences and backgrounds contribute to a fuller, more robust plan for the future.

Moreover, embracing adaptability and building on the learning from past experiences equip teams to face future challenges with resilience. This proactiveness ensures that the team is not derailed by unforeseen setbacks but can navigate them with agility and confidence. Learning from the past, while maintaining a forward-facing perspective, anchors the team in reality but sets its sights on new horizons.

However, envisioning the future state is not enough. A team must break down its long-term objectives into short-term, actionable initiatives. These become performance benchmarks that guide day-to-day activities and ensure that everyone is moving in the right direction. Regular reviews of these benchmarks help the team stay on track and make necessary adjustments, ensuring that the ambitions remain within reach.

It is also crucial to herald not just the destination but the journey itself. Recognizing and valuing the incremental progress made towards achieving a future goal sustains motivation. Small victories are precious; they are the thread that weaves the larger tapestry of success.

Celebrating these moments reinforces unity and reinforces the belief that every step forward is an achievement in its own right.

Finally, to cultivate a lasting culture of growth and achievement, it is essential to foster an environment that values continuous learning. Teams that prioritize development and skill enhancement find that they are better equipped to handle the evolving demands of their environment. By remaining lifelong learners, team members ensure that the collective expertise of the group is always expanding, keeping them at the cutting edge of performance.

Future planning, when done as a team, becomes more than a series of objectives to hit; it becomes a shared journey of growth, learning, and achievement. It transforms the essence of work from a mere function of necessity to a purpose-driven pursuit of excellence where every member contributes to something greater than themselves.

This forward momentum, powered by collective ambition and nurtured through thoughtful planning, is what propels teams beyond the ordinary. It facilitates a cycle of success that promises not only to reach current goals but also to lay the groundwork for new achievements in a future that the team builds together.

Chapter 13:
The Ripple Effect of Teamwork

As we reflect upon the journey traversed through these chapters, we understand that the essence of true collaboration is far-reaching and transformative. Upon the robust framework of trust, dedicated communication, and mutual respect, teams are not just vessels of collective effort but powerful catalysts for change. Like a pebble cast into a pond, the impact of teamwork extends outward, influencing not only the immediate goals at hand but creating waves that touch the shores of larger organizational success, community well-being, and individual fulfillment.

The synergy of a unified team brings forth a strength much greater than the sum of individual efforts. Within these dynamics, we've seen how shared goals and visions encourage each member to rise above personal triumphs, to contribute their unique strengths for the greater good. In doing so, teams become breeding grounds for innovation, resilience, and adaptability, turning the gears of progress with unwavering commitment and collective intellect.

Moreover, the power of teamwork extends beyond the walls of meetings and project timelines. It influences our approach toward conflict, urging us to view tensions as opportunities to forge stronger bonds and achieve greater understandings. Here, in the crucible of disagreement, teams can unearth solutions that not only resolve immediate issues but also set the stage for enduring harmony and shared success. Embracing diversity within teams propels this even further, allowing the confluence of varied insights to sculpt a more robust and all-encompassing strategy for success.

And let us not forget, the resonance of positive teamwork reverberates through the very culture of an organization, inspiring leadership and commitment at every level. A team that moves with a singular pulse fosters an environment where individuals are valued, heard, and propelled to grow. This atmosphere of support and recognition does not only achieve targets but also nurtures the seeds for future leaders and innovators who will continue to push the boundaries of what can be achieved collectively.

Finally, as our exploration of teamwork culminates, it is evident that the ripple effect is perpetual. Each achievement, each milestone celebrated, and each adversity overcome serves as a stepping stone to new horizons. The legacy of a well-harmonized team is etched into the annals of its accomplishments and the personal growth of its members. For those who dare to invest in the power of togetherness, the rewards are boundless, echoing through the annals of their endeavors and beyond, into the vast potential of what they can achieve together.

Appendix A:
Inspirational Quotes on Teamwork

Emerging from the vast exploration of what forms the backbone of collective success, we now pause to reflect on the distilled wisdom of those who have articulated the power of togetherness. Let these curated words on teamwork serve not merely as a source of inspiration but as a guidepost reminding us that the strength of the team lies within the unity of its members.

On Collaborative Spirit

- "Individual commitment to a group effort - that is what makes a team work, a company work, a society work, a civilization work." - Unattributed

- "Talent wins games, but teamwork and intelligence win championships." - Unattributed

- "Alone we can do so little; together we can do so much." - Unattributed

On Shared Goals and Vision

1. "A vision becomes a milestone when the whole team sees where they're heading and join forces to get there." - Unattributed

2. "Success is best when it's shared." - Unattributed

On Diversity and Unity

- "Diversity is not about how we differ. Diversity is about embracing one another's uniqueness." - Unattributed

- "We may have all come on different ships, but we're in the same boat now." - Unattributed

On Leadership and Empowerment

1. "Leaders become great, not because of their power, but because of their ability to empower others." - Unattributed

2. "Good leaders must first become good servants." - Unattributed

On Trust and Dependability

- "Trust is the glue of life. It's the foundational principle that holds all relationships." - Unattributed

- "When a team trusts each other, and when we have each other's back, we are unstoppable." - Unattributed

On Challenges and Resilience

1. "It is literally true that you can succeed best and quickest by helping others to succeed." - Unattributed

2. "The strength of the team is each individual member. The strength of each member is the team." - Unattributed

On Motivation and Encouragement

- "A successful team is a group of many hands but of one mind." - Unattributed

- "Teamwork is the secret that makes common people achieve uncommon results." - Unattributed

May these words resonate, igniting the spark of teamwork within you. As you go forth, remember that the synergy of a unified team can transform the greatest of visions into tangible achievements. In the essence of collaboration, celebrate every contribution, and foster an environment where every member's potential is recognized and nurtured. Together, we can create a scenario in which everyone wins—an embodiment of true teamwork.

Appendix B:
Practical Exercises for Team Building

Introduction to Team Building Exercises

Throughout the journey to strengthen any team, it is crucial to engage in practical exercises that not only hone skills but also forge the bonds that are essential for a unified and resilient group. These activities are designed to highlight the importance of communication, trust, and mutual support, traits that transform a collection of individuals into a powerful collective force. Below, you will find a range of hands-on exercises tailored to instill these attributes and reinforce the power of togetherness for shared success.

Exercise 1: The Trust Fall

The classic 'Trust Fall' is much more than an icebreaker; it symbolizes the essence of reliance and faith in one another.

1. Participants partner up, with one person being the 'faller' and the other the 'catcher'.

2. The faller stands with their back to the catcher, crosses their arms over their chest, and falls backward without bending their knees.

3. The catcher's role is to catch the faller, confirming their commitment to support their teammate.

4. After each fall, partners swap roles and repeat the process.

Exercise 2: Blind Drawing

This exercise enhances communication and interpretation skills, indispensable tools for achieving shared goals.

1. Divide the team into pairs, with one member as the 'director' and the other as the 'drawer'.

2. Drawers are given a blank piece of paper and a pen but must keep their eyes closed or be blindfolded.

3. Directors have a picture or shape that the drawer must replicate, but they can only use verbal instructions to guide the drawer.

4. After a set time, groups compare the original image to the drawn one, discussing the clarity of communication and ways to improve.

Exercise 3: The Minefield

In this exercise, teams navigate an obstacle course, improving their strategic planning and trust.

1. Create a 'minefield' by placing objects sporadically across a large area – indoors or outdoors.

2. Team members work in pairs. One is blindfolded, the other must verbally guide them through the minefield without stepping on any objects.

3. If the blindfolded person touches an object, they must start over. The goal is to cross the minefield with the least amount of errors.

Exercise 4: Problem-Solving Scenarios

Engage teams with scenarios that require collaboration, creative thinking, and the ability to leverage diverse perspectives for innovative solutions.

1. Divide the team into small groups and provide each with a different complex scenario that requires a solution.

2. Each team has a set time to brainstorm and present their plan of action.

3. After presentations, teams reflect on how they worked together, valuing everyone's input and how they achieved their end goal.

Exercise 5: Tower Building Contest

This activity ignites the competitive spirit while emphasizing the need for team input and cooperative strategy.

1. Provide each team with the same set of materials (e.g., sticks, tape, straws, and a marshmallow).

2. Teams are challenged to build the highest free-standing tower with the marshmallow on top within a time limit.

3. After completion, teams can discuss what strategies worked, how leadership emerged, and the importance of coordinating diverse ideas.

Closing Thoughts on Team Building Exercises

These practical exercises offer a glimpse into how dynamic team building can enhance individual capacities while, more importantly, creating a supportive network of collaboration and mutual achievement. Whether dealing with the foundational aspects of trust or the intricate dynamics of problem-solving, the exercises selected in this appendix serve to highlight and practice the principles put forth in the preceding chapters. They are not just activities, but opportunities for growth, understanding, and the celebration of human interdependence.

Utilizing these team building exercises can lead to a significant shift in the way individuals perceive their roles within a team and foster an environment where each success is felt by all. This shared experience is a powerful catalyst for change, driving teams to strive for excellence through collective effort and mutual support. With each exercise and reflection, teams can transform the potential of togetherness into tangible success, creating win-win scenarios that are both fulfilling and lasting.

Appendix C:
Resources for Further Reading

The journey of enhancing ourselves and forging bonds of togetherness is a continuous one, and the pursuit of knowledge is never complete. This appendix is dedicated to those who seek to dive deeper into the realms of teamwork, leadership, and personal growth. Below is a curated selection of resource materials that will serve as a beacon for your ongoing quest of self-improvement and collaboration in creating win-win scenarios. Each resource has been chosen for its potential to inspire and enlighten your path toward collective triumph.

Books on Teamwork and Collaboration

- *The Five Dysfunctions of a Team: A Leadership Fable* - A gripping exploration of the challenges teams face and how to overcome them to function cohesively.

- *Drive: The Surprising Truth About What Motivates Us* - Provides insights into the motivations that fuel our collective drive in team settings.

- *Synergy: The Unique Relationship Between Nurses and Patients* - Conveys the power of teamwork in high-stakes environments and its outcomes on impacting lives.

- *The Wisdom of Teams: Creating the High-Performance Organization* - Shares essential knowledge on how teams work and how they can become more effective.

Insightful Articles on Leadership

1. "Leadership That Gets Results" - Delving into various leadership styles and their direct impact on team dynamics and performance.

2. "Cultivating Leadership in Teams: An Essential Ingredient for Success" - Explores how leadership at all levels contributes to a team's success.

3. "Leadership's Ripple Effect: How Small Actions Can Impact Large Systems" - Reveals the significance of every leadership action and its broader implications.

Journals and Periodicals

For those who prefer to stay updated with the latest research and discussions in the fields of teamwork and leadership, consider subscribing to industry-specific journals and periodicals such as:

- *The Harvard Business Review* - Offers a wealth of knowledge with articles on management, leadership, and teamwork.

- *The Journal of Team Performance Management* - An academic journal focusing on the latest findings in team dynamics and performance.

Podcasts and Talks

If absorbing wisdom through listening fits your lifestyle better, these thought-provoking podcasts and lecture series will provide a well of inspiration and innovation:

- "The Power of Vulnerability" - A series that discusses the crucial role of vulnerability and trust in building strong, resilient teams.

- "WorkLife with Adam Grant" - Covers a range of topics from individual motivation to the secrets of resilient teams.

- "Leading Teams: Insights from Google's Project Aristotle" - A revealing look into what makes teams effective at one of the world's most innovative companies.

May these resources spark a greater understanding and appreciation of the power of coming together, the strength of shared visions, and the enduring impact of collective efforts. As you immerse in these works, remember that every page turned, every idea considered, and each perspective understood can be a stepping stone towards a future where success and togetherness are intertwined.

About The Author

D r. Rajan Gupta was born and brought up in New Delhi, India. His childhood was in the city of Delhi. He came across many people in his life who have helped shape his present. Every single person who came in his life whether he or she gave good or bad experiences to him, he believes was an important person otherwise his life would not have been the same. So, he is thankful to everyone. He believes that attachments and detachments with people or anything in life are timed and destined. One of the most memorable things for him from childhood was a quote written by his father on a mantlepiece "Ishwar aur maut ko kabhi mat bhulo" means "never forget God and Death.

After schooling he went to Ahmedabad for his medical school. This was one of the most beautiful phases of his life where he created so many beautiful relations of his life. Later he traveled to USA and received residency training at St Francis Medical Center (UPMC) in Pittsburgh and his Intervention Pain fellowship at Vanderbilt University in Nashville (Tennessee). Dr. Gupta has been practicing pain management for over 10 years and has his practices in South Jersey and Philadelphia. He has received multiple awards including the "Best Hands" award for intervention pain, Top Doctor award in 2015, 2016, 2017,2018, 2019, South Jersey Magazine Top Physicians award in 2017, 2018, 2019,2020, 2021, 2022, 2023, The Philadelphia Magazine Top Physician award 2018, 2019, 2020, 2021, 2022, 2023 the Prestigious Pillar of Community Service award in 2013 and many more.

He has been a writer all his life. He loves to create things. He has written The Briefcase Life, Carry what matters the most....., "7 ways in 7 days to change your life", "Growing to be pain free", Surviving Corona, and is currently working on "Married with Pain" and "3SSS in a successful relationship", and "How to be a modern Buddha". He has also acted, and produced movies like "Cozy Connections", "The Beginning of the End" based on the principles of his books. He believes that contentment is the key. Whatever you do, whatever you have, just be content with it. That will bring peace. Pain and sufferings are inevitable. He says to follow the laws of his books as filters so that you can "Stop Suffering and Start Living".

www.ingramcontent.com/pod-product-compliance
Lightning Source LLC
Chambersburg PA
CBHW022004170526
45157CB00003B/1133